FRANCE IS NOW V

There has never been a vegetarian guide to France like this one. It features wonderful vegetarian restaurants, cafés, hotels and gîtes all over France with:

Le vin

- opening times
- complete addresses
- phone and fax numbers
- prices
- detailed descriptions
- what's on the menu for vegans
- clear directions

Whether you're hankering for a weekend trip or touring the country, a student seeking a bargain buffet or looking for luxury, now you can be sure of finding fabulous French vegetarian food wherever you go.

Co-author **Alex Bourke** worked for a major guidebook publisher from 1985 to 1989 and wrote *The Vegan Guide to Paris* and bestsellling *Vegetarian London*. **Alan Todd** is a publishing consultant for green charities such as Forum for the Future and The International Hotels Environment Initiative. They have also published *Vegetarian Britain*.

"From Paris to Perpignan, everywhere you need to know for a perfect night out, weekend or holiday."
Tina Fox, Chief Executive, The Vegetarian Society

"An invaluable guide to finding really good vegetarian food." - **Paul and Linda McCartney**

Vegetarian France. ISBN 1-902259 00 9.
by Alex Bourke and AlanTodd. Foreword by Paul & Linda
McCartney. Introduction by Roselyne Masselin.
First published March 1998 by Vegetarian Guides Ltd, 197
Greyhound Road, London W14 9SD

Cover designed by Mark Halunga, 0171-794 1149
Paris map by Marc Vyvyan-Jones. Vignettes by Philippa Pettet.
French edition *Le guide des restaurant végétariens de France*, ISBN 2-84221-031-X published by Éditions La Page, 37 boulevard Diderot BP 150, 75562 Paris Cedex 12, France.

UK and worldwide distributor: Central Books, 99 Wallis
Road, London E9 5LN, England. Tel 0181-986 4854, Fax
0181-533 5821. Available in France from Éditions La Plage,

Also published simultaneously:
Vegetarian Britain, £7.99, ISBN 1-902259 01 7

In preparation: *Vegetarian Belgium and Holland*

Individual copies available from the publishers. See order form at the end of this guide.

The small print:

Printed and bound in Great Britain by
Cox & Wyman Ltd. Reading, Berkshire

VEGETARIAN
FRANCE

over 150 places to eat and sleep

by Alex Bourke and Alan Todd

Foreword by Paul & Linda McCartney

Introduction by Roselyne Masselin
of La Cuisine Imaginaire

published by Vegetarian Guides, London
in association with Éditions La Plage, Paris

CONTENTS

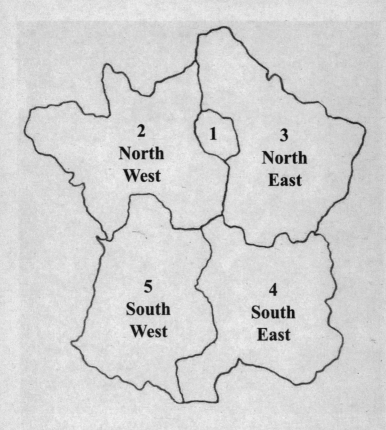

We have based the areas on the French telephone system. All numbers are 8 digits, prefixed with the digit 1 for Paris and Ile de France, 2 for North West etc. When dialling from UK, prefix the nine digit number listed with 00-33. When dialling within France, just dial the last 8 digits if you're in that area, otherwise prefix the 9 digit number with a zero.

Foreword

by

Paul & Linda McCartney

A lot of people think it's impossible to find vegetarian food in France, but this little cracker of a book proves them wrong. *Vegetarian France* is an invaluable guide to finding really good vegetarian food in the most unexpected places.

Bon appetit!

BIG Merci from Alex et Alan to:

Alex at MPL, Aneeta, Laurence Auger, Geoff Baker, Dirk Boeckx, Mike Bourke, Steve Connor, Eric Cooper, Jean-Luc Ferrante, Tina Fox, Francis, Dr Michael Grill, Mark Halunga, Shelagh Jones, Jean-François Leménicier, Amanda Martin, Huong Nguyen, Ian Kirby, Paul and Linda McCartney, Pierre, Doug Robertson, Dr Kasia Siudem, Philippa Pettet, Marc Vyvyan-Jones, Avery Wham, Yasmin, and all our friends & supporters.

Vegetarian guides charges NOTHING to be listed in our guides. We wrote to everyone listed in the book that we could not visit in person. Those who ignored our generous offer of free publicity we harassed mercilessly till they finally sent their menus. And we asked local veggie gastronauts what they reckoned too. Anywhere with minimal listings proved impossible to get a reply from. But you're welcome to it next time around.... just return our questionnaire or your menu!

Vive la France!

French born **Roselyne Masselin** is the founder of **La Cuisine Imaginaire** cookery school and **Catering Imaginaire Catering Company** and author of **Classic BBC Cuisine Imaginaire - the ultimate guide for vegetarian entertaining**. She appears frequently on TV and radio with features in the press and magazines such as BBC Vegetarian Good Food.

We French gave the world the words gourmet, café and joie de vivre, not to mention soufflé, casserole, apéritif, hors d'oeuvre, sauté, patisserie, profiterole and dozens more. French has always been the language of haute cuisine, unless you're a végétarien ... until now! With this book in your pocket you'll find that France is a veritable veggie or vegan paradise.

Much of Britain is barren, treeless farmland grazing animals or growing fodder. France, which is twice the size, has huge areas of real countryside, forests, mountains, and thousands of kilometres of fabulous coastline. Farms and vineyards tend to be family run with fresh, often organic, food that goes straight from the field or orchard to the local market to your table.

This guide contains lovely country guest houses run by vegetarians, some of them British, and there are many inexpensive gîtes, independent flats or cottages with a kitchen.

French vegetarian restaurants offer bright, crunchy salads, rich and tempting dishes based on traditional grains, pulses, and locally grown vegetables plus tofu or tempeh. Desserts range from super-healthy to downright devilish - after all, you are on holiday. You'll be delighted by fresh juices, from carrot to grape, and of course all kinds of wine, many organic, at a fraction of UK prices. Veggie restaurants are often tucked away in cobbled sidestreets, away from the tourist throngs, peaceful, enchanting, an oasis of good food where you can linger for an hour or three. There are also many ethnic restaurants and grocers with your favourite dishes such as North African couscous, Middle Eastern meze, Oriental stir fries and of course curry.

Lunch in France is never less than an hour. Why hurry? Enjoy a soya milkshake or something stronger, two or three courses followed by real coffee in the company of family. Even at work, the one hour lunch break is observed religiously. Your workmates are also your friends.

The French start their day with warm baguettes and croissants of all kinds, even chococate ones and vegan croissants from the Jewish bakeries in the Marais district of Paris. Between meals you can relax in pavement cafés drinking herb tea or a glass of beer or wine, savouring the ambience and the aroma of coffee and freshly-baked bread. All restaurants and cafés are now smoke-free with a separate smoking section.

Wholefood stores, supermarkets and street markets sell everything you need for self-catering or un picnic from peaches to peanut butter. You'll find all your favourite grains and nuts, locally grown fruit and vegetables far fresher than you're used to - from aubergines to oranges, smoked tofu or scrumptious banana flavoured soya milk. Vegans will delight in the dark chocolate available everywhere and several yummy flavours of Sojasun yoghurts.

Whether touring by car, bus, railpass, foot or thumb, France offers you the holiday of a lifetime, right on the doorstep of Britain. Even though I run a demanding business, I still find time to visit my Normandy homeland several times a year. Once you've joined the nine million British who go to France every year, no doubt like me you'll want to return at every opportunity.

It only remains for me to wish you Bon Voyage et Bon Appetit!

Roselyne Masselin

Roselyne Masselin's Vegetarian (and Vegan) Services
PO Box 70, Bushey, Herts WD2 2NQ, England.
Tel 01923-250099. Fax 01923-250030.

PARLEZ-VOUS VEGGIE?

Whether you're a total débutant or have a French degree, there's always more to learn.

Alex highly recommends Berlitz phrasebooks and the accompanying cassette. Get one a few months before you go and listen while walking or driving around for half an hour a day. Even if you have a French degree, you'll still enjoy the specialist sections that others can save for emergencies.

There are several dietary systems popular in France, notably **Dr Kousmine**, which is famous for its breakfast concoction Crème Budwig. **Macrobiotics** is based on Japanese wholefoods featuring seitan (wheat gluten fake meat), tempeh, tofu, locally grown grains plus brown rice, seaweed (des algues) like wakame and gomasio (ground sesame with salt).

Here's some specialist vocab to supplement your phrase book.

auberge de jeunesse	youth hostel
J'aimerais...	I'd like...
ne pas déranger	do not disturb
issue de secours	emergency exit
le rez-de-chaussée	ground floor
le sous-sol	basement
Je suis végétarien(ne)	I'm a vegetarian
Je suis végétalien(ne)	I'm a vegan
Biologique, bio	organic

Le Champignon

Cassoulet

La Baguette

de l'ail	garlic	le maïs	maize, corn
un ananas	pineapple	le marron	chestnut
artichauts	artichokes		
les asperges	asparagus	*la noix*	*nut, walnut*
une assiette	plate	*la noisette*	*nut, hazelnut*
avoine	oats	*une amande*	*almond*
les azukis	aduki beans	*le cajou*	*cashew nut*
la banane	banana	*la cacah(o)uète*	*peanut*
bavarois	fruit mousse	*beurre d'arachides*	*peanut butter*
le beignet	fritter	*(or beurre de cacahouètes)*	
le blé	wheat	*le pignon*	*pine nut*
une boîte	box, tin	*le pavot*	*poppy seed*
le boulghur	bulgur-wheat		
le cassoulet	casserole	orge (f)	barley
céreales	grains	le pain complet	wholemeal bread
la cérise	cherry	pain au son	wholemeal bread
crudités	green salad		(bran)
le magasin	health food shop	pain cinq céreales	five grain bread
diététique		pain de seigle	rye bread
de l'épinard	spinach	les pâtes	pasta
une escalope	steak/burger	(sans oeufs)	(without eggs)
farci	stuffed	la pêche	peach
les fraises	strawberries	les pois chiches	chick peas
fruits secs	dried fruit	le potage/la soupe	soup
la galette	flat pastry cake	le potimarron	pumpkin, squash
les germes	seeds, sprouts	quinoa	South American
germes de soja	breansprouts		grain
le gluten	gluten	le riz	rice
sans gluten	gluten free	le soja	soya
sans graisse	without animal fat	tamari/shoyu	soya sauce
animale		tapenade	olive paté
le légume	vegetable	la truffe	truffle
des lentilles	lentils	à vapeur	steamed
la levure	yeast		

Le vin

Biologique

La Bière

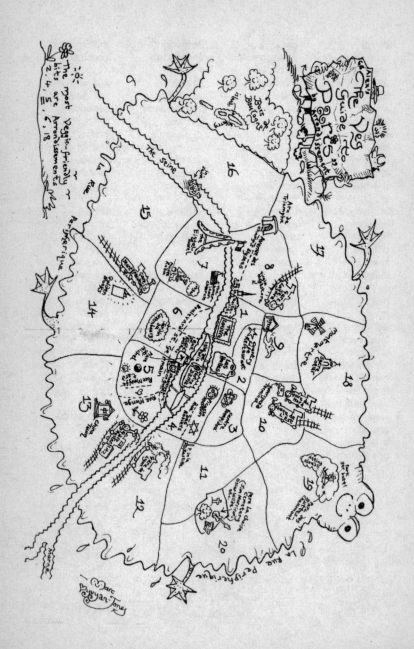

1. PARIS

1st arrondissement

Entre Ciel et Terre

Restaurant. Vegetarian.
Entre Ciel et Terre (Twixt Heaven and Earth)
5 rue Hérold
Tel: 1-45 08 49 84
Métro: Les Halles, Louvre-Rivoli, Bourse.
Bus: 29 - 67 - 85 - 74 (stop Louvre/Etienne-Marcel)
Non-smoking. Seats 38.
Right in the heart of Paris, not far from Place des Victoires, the
Louvre Post Office and the St. Eustache church.
Open noon to 3 p.m. and 7 to 10 p.m. Monday to Friday. Closed in
August. Booking advised.
Credit cards: CB, Visa.
This restaurant, established by Guillaume Botte in 1988, tries to raise
simple vegetarian cookery to a more heavenly level (hence the name
of the restaurant). Its efforts have been been successful, since, after
first getting a mention in Gault and Millau, it has now been included in
the 1997 Michelin Guide.
In a tastefully decorated room, where works of art hang on the walls,
you have a choice of menus: two at lunchtime for 69F & 87F, one in
the evening for 87F, a plat du jour (daily special), a tarte du jour (the
dessert special), or a meal à la carte for which you should allow
between 100F and 150F.
Specialities include: tapenade maison ('olive paste') served with
Poilane (fried) bread and hard boiled egg 43F, taboulé à la milanaise
(Milan tabouleh) 27F, tarte aux carottes et à la menthe fraîche (carrot
tart with fresh mint) 54F, galettes de céreale accompagnées de
légumes (cereal burgers and vegetables) 56F, lasagne 55F, gateau
aux pommes, figues et cannnelle (apple, fig and cinnamon cake) 32F,
gâteau aux poires et pépites de chocolat et sa crème anglaise (pear
and chocolate chip gateau with custard) 32F.
Wines from 43F to 87F a bottle, but also pétillant de raisin (sparkling

grape juice), fresh fruit juices, coffee substitute.
About 50% of the food is organic. Vegans are catered for. Neither
meat nor fish is served.
Also: take-away, food shop, bookshop and cookery courses available.
Catering service.

La Victoire Suprême du Coeur

Restaurant. Vegetarian.
La Victoire Suprême du Coeur
41 rue des Bourdonnais
Tel: 1-40 41 93 95
near the Forum des Halles
Métro: Châtelet - Les Halles
Bus: 38 - 47 - 75 - 74 - 85
Summer terrace.
Non-smoking, seating 60, wheelchair access.
Open noon to 10pm non stop Monday to Saturday, closed Sunday.
Closed the second week of April and the second fortnight of August.
Visa, Euro & MasterCard accepted.
A group of friends who share common spiritual aims, offer vegetarian
and vegan menus from 49F to 78F at lunchtime and 78F in the
evening. A la carte for between 79F and 130F.
Also: take-away, bookshop and cookery courses.

2nd arrondissement

Country Life

Restaurant with self-service buffet. Vegan.
6 rue Danou
Tel: 01-42 97 48 51
Open: Mon-Fri 12-14.30, Mon-Thu 19-22.00. Closed Sat-Sun
Métro: Opéra - RER : Auber
Bus: 20-42-52-81-68-29-95-22-53-66-21
Non-smoking.
Located near the Opera, this large self-service restaurant is on the
first floor, above a shop selling natural produce.
One price only, 67F, for which vegetarians and vegans may take their

pick from among 18 fresh salad, vegetable and hot grain and bean dishes plus soup in this superb value all-you-can-eat vegan buffet restaurant. Desserts are extra (vegans should watch out for honey in some), as are fruit juices, carrot juices and mineral waters.

20% of the ingredients are organic and the bread comes from a small-scale bakery.

Also: take-away, health food shop, book section, and cookery courses.

Country Life is enormously popular with vegans visiting Paris. If you want more of the same, check out Country Life in Warwick Street, London W1. (See our companion guides *Vegetarian Britain* and *Vegetarian London*)

4th arrondissement

Aquarius

Restaurant. Vegetarian.
54 rue Sainte-Croix-de-la-Bretonnerie
Tel: 1-48 87 48 71
Near Beaubourg, Pompidou Centre
Métro: Hôtel de Ville. RER: Châtelet-les-Halles.
Bus: 67-69-76-96-63-74-72-75
Non-smoking, seating 50, wheelchair access.
Open: noon - 10pm, Monday to Thursday. Noon - 10.30pm Friday and Saturday.
Credit cards: Visa, MasterCard, Eurocard.
Located in the Marais district, Aquarius is a co-operative owned by the staff since 1974. Apparently not a bad set up since a second restaurant was opened in 1981, also in Paris, in the 14th arrondissement. (see further on in this guide)
The decor is rustic with solid wooden tables and 70% of the food served is organic.
There is a choice of two menus for 56F or 84F, or à la carte about 70F for a meal, including tabouleh, pâté végétal aux champignons (vegetable paté with mushrooms), gratin de légumes (vegetable bake), assiette paysanne (mixed platter), tourte (pie), gâteau au chocolat (chocolate cake).
There are dishes modified for vegans, notably the speciality of the

day (le plat du jour), for children la galette de blé avec des pommes de terre roties (wheat burgers with roast potatoes).
Neither meat nor fish is served.
To accompany your meal: pain complet (wholemeal bread), cidre bio (organic cider), jus de fruits ou de légumes maisons (fruit juices or their own vegetable juices), organic Bordeaux wine (60F a bottle, 20F for a pitcher), or quite simply water (purified by reverse osmosis filtration) which is on the table.
Also: take-away, health food shop, bookshop, talks about Rosicrucianism.

Chez Julien

Restaurant. Vegetarian-friendly.
1 rue du pont Louis-Philippe
Tel: 1-42 78 31 64
Near the Hôtel de Ville.
Métro: Pont Marie
Bus: 67-69-76-96
Seating 45
Open: noon to 2pm and 7.30 to 11pm.
Closed Sunday and lunchtimes on Monday and Saturday.
Credit cards accepted.
Vegetarians will easily find something to their taste on the menu. Starters include nid de tagliatelles a la fleur de basilic (nest of tagliatelle with basil) 65F; fricassée de champignons a la provençale (Provencal mushroom fricassée) 75F. Main course might be chou farci aux légumes variés (cabbage stuffed with a variety of vegetables) 110F.

L'Ébouillante

Restaurant. Vegetarian-friendly.
L'Ébouillante
6 rue des Barres
Tel: 1-42 71 09 69
Behind the Hôtel de Ville.
Métro: Hôtel de Ville, Saint-Paul, or Pont Marie.
Bus: 67-96-69-76-72-74-47
Seating 50, wheelchair access, outside tables in the summer.

Open: noon to 10pm Tuesday to Sunday. Closed Monday.
In a pedestrianised street, this traditional restaurant is pleasant for
outdoor dining in the summer.
Vegetarians are catered for with ten kinds of vegetable or feta-based
bakes, prices ranging from 42F to 58F.

Le Grand Appétit

Restaurant. Vegetarian-friendly.
9 rue de la Cerisaie
Tel: 1-40 27 04 95
Fax: 1-44 59 81 75
Near the Place de la Bastille.
Métro: Bastille
Bus: 20-65-29-86-87-69-76-74-91
Vegetarian restaurant, seating 30, non-smoking, wheelchair access.
Open: noon to 3 p.m.
Closed: Saturday, and for ten days in March/April.
Credit cards: Visa.
This vegetarian restaurant, established in 1986, is situated at the
back of a shop with the same name selling natural produce. There is
no set menu but a choice of dishes from 35F to 100F, almost entirely
organic.
Madame David, the chef, will introduce you to ingredients typical of
macrobiotic cuisine. You have the choice of miso soup, potage de
céréales ou de légumes (grain or vegetable soup), l'assiette complète
(the full monty) 59F with céréales (cereals/grains), légumes cuits ou
crus (cooked or fresh vegetables), tofu or seitan. For dessert, compote (stewed fruit), gâteau or custard tart.
The infusion (herb tea) of the day is free, but you may also choose
from saké, bière (beer), jus de pomme ou de légumes (apple or vegetable juice), thés (teas), and coffee.
No meat or fish are served.
Also: take-away, health food shop, bookshop and cookery courses.

La Bière

Piccolo Teatro

Restaurant. Vegetarian.
6 rue des Écouffes
Tel: 1-42 72 17 19
In the Marais district.
Métro: Saint-Paul
Bus: 67-69-76-96
Vegetarian restaurant, non-smoking, seating 40, wheelchair access.
Open: noon to 3 p.m. and 7 - 11 p.m.
Closed: Mondays and in August.
Booking advised.
Credit cards: Visa and American Express.
Opened in 1976 as a tearoom, it became a vegetarian restaurant in 1986 started by Alain Liang.
Located in a 17th century house, very typical of the Marais district, near the Hotel de Ville, it offers lunchtime menus at 45F to 53F and evening menus at 90F to 115F. For an à la carte meal reckon on about 90F excluding drinks.
They serve gratins, vegetable dishes topped with cheese, or for vegans Ursula Muller offers macrobiotic-inspired cuisine. The specialities of the house are pâté végétal (vegetable paté), vegetarian moussaka, and red fruit crumble. Also Poilane wholemeal bread.
50% of the food is organic, notably the wine.
Also: take-away.

Rami et Hanna

Restaurant. Vegetarian-friendly.
Rami et Hanna
54 rue des Rosiers
Tel: 1-42 78 23 09
Near the Musée Picasso.
Métro: Saint-Paul or Hôtel de Ville
Bus: 69-76-96
Seating 34
Open: noon to 2 am.
Booking advised for Saturday or Sunday.
Credit cards accepted.
Here in the Jewish quarter of the Rue des Rosiers, beloved of

tourists, you will find the most luxurious take-away falafels ever, consisting of pitta bread filled with deep fried chickpea balls, fresh vegetables, hummous and tahini sauce, all topped with a magical slice of fried aubergine, for around 25F.

Eating in, you can discover Israeli cooking, rich in vegetarian dishes. Hanna offers: hummus 31F, aubergines in a spicy sauce 35F, beignets de pommes de terre (potato fritters) 19F, falafel 39F with the ingredients laid out ready for you to construct your own pitta sandwich or just eat like mezze. Wash it all down with le thé a la menthe (mint tea) 16F, Vittel mineral water 12F, or a bottle of wine 80F.

La Truffe

Restaurant. Vegetarian.
31 rue Vieille-du-Temple
Tel: 1-42 71 08 39
In the Marais district at the western end of rue des Rosiers.
Métro: Hotel de Ville or Saint-Paul
Bus: 29-75-69-76-96-67
Seating 40, wheelchair access.
Open: noon to 3 pm, and 6 to 11 pm
Tea-room: 3 to 6 pm.
Closed: Mondays, also late August, early September.
Credit cards: Visa, MasterCard.
This top class vegetarian restaurant, popular with music and film stars like Vanessa Paradis, offers you, in a pleasing stone, wood and glass environment, a set menu for 59F (lunchtime only) and dishes à la carte from 35F to 129F. Mushroom and truffle based dishes are the house speciality of the charming vegan owner Marianna. Also vegetable terrine, tiramisù, tarte au chocolat.
Most dishes, even the desserts, are vegan.
Neither meat nor fish are served.
About 70% of the food is organic, notably the bread, the wine, the beer, and the champagne.
Booking essential in the evening.
Also: take-away, small bookshop, tea-room.

Le Champignon

5th arrondissement

Le Grenier de Notre Dame

Restaurant. Vegetarian.
18 rue de la Bûcherie
Tel: 1-44 32 99 829
On the left bank, near Notre-Dame.
Métro: Saint-Michel.
Bus: 24-63-86-87-85-38-21-96
Seating 60, with one room for non-smokers and one for smokers, outside tables in summer.
Open: noon to 2.30 pm and 7 to 11.30 pm. Booking advised weekends and in summer.
Credit cards accepted.
On the left bank opposite Notre Dame, and close to the English bookshop Shakespeare & Co, where they have been for the past 18 years. The Grenier de Notre-Dame offers a vegetarian and organic cuisine in a rustic setting with exposed beams. At midday and in the evening there are three set menus for 75F, 105F and 78F. The one at 78F is designed to allow the uninitated to discover vegetarian cuisine. For a meal à la carte allow about 130F.
Specialities include Cassoulet végétarien (vegetable stew) 79F, Lasagnes végétariennes (veg lasagne) 60F, couscous, gratin de légumes (veg with cheese on top) and macrobiotic dishes. All washed down with organic wine sold by the glass, the carafe or the bottle.
Also: take-away and a small food shop.

La Petite Légume

Restaurant
Vegetarian
36 rue des Boulangers
Tel: 1-40 46 06 85
Near the Arènes de Lutèce, the Contrescarpe and Jussieu University.
Métro: Cardinal Lemoine or Jussieu.
Bus: 47-67-89.
Seating 30, non-smoking, wheelchair access, with outside tables in

the summer.
Open: Noon to 2.30pm and 7.30 to 10pm. Closed Sunday. Booking
advised for groups.
Credit cards: Visa, CB, American Express & Mastercard accepted.
In this shop-restaurant Patricia Roffay and her husband offer 3 set
menus at lunchtime (50F, 64F & 75F) and meals à la carte at
lunchtime and in the evening. Dishes (from 28F to 65F) are, as far as
possible, prepared with organic ingredients.
Together with the great variety of condiments available, you may
choose for example; tarte aux légumes et au fromage de chèvre (vegetable tart with goat's cheese) 33F, choucroute aux saucisses végé-
tales (sauerkraut and veg. sausages) 58F, couscous 58F, or the
desserts of the house: gâteau bio (organic gateau) 32F, flan aux fruits
secs (dried fruit flan) 19F, washed down with a jus de fruit (fruit juice)
or a jus de légumes (vegetable juice) each 16F, or tea or wine.
Vegan macrobiotic dishes are offered, likewise fish.
Also: take-away, shop selling natural produce, bookshop.

Les Quatre et Une Saveurs

Restaurant. Vegetarian.
72 rue du Cardinal-Lemoine
Tel: 1-43 26 88 80
Near the Arènes de Lutèce
Métro: Cardinal Lemoine or Monge
Bus: 89-63-86-87-67-24
Non-smoking, seating 40 with 2 or 3 tables outside.
Open: Noon to 3pm and 7.15 to 10.30pm (11pm in summer). Closed
on Monday.
The decor is Mediterranean with bamboo blinds, seed-decorated
tables, bright colours... and the cooking is very much macrobiotic.
Here you will find a set menu for 68F: it comprises a Japanese box
containing a complete meal (cereals, vegetables, seaweed, tofu or
seitan or tempeh). The meal changes every day. You may also opt
for the 120F menu (the Japanese box has a vegetable or miso soup),
followed by a dessert and tea or barley-coffee.
The food is organic. A fish dish is also on offer every day. There is an
organic wine list, also fresh juices.
Also: take-away.

Au Jardin des Pâtes

Restaurant. Vegetarian.
4 rue Lacepède
Tel: 1-43 31 50 71
Fax: 01 45 35 42 12
In the middle of the Latin quarter, near the Jardin des Plantes.
Métro: Jussieu, or Place Monge.
Bus: 67-47
Seating 30, outside tables in summer.
Open: noon to 2.30 pm and 7 to 11 p.m. Tuesday to Sunday.
Closed: Mondays, and in August.
Booking advised.
Credit cards accepted.
Here everything is prepared on the premises. The grains are whole-meal and organic, stone-ground daily to provide flour that is really fresh and nutritious. There is a choice of dishes made from rice flour, wheat flour, barley flour, rye flour, buckwheat flour, even chestnut flour ... garnished with laitue de mer (a type of seaweed), poireaux fondus (glazed leeks), champignons (mushrooms), pruneaux (prunes), with prices from 38F to 73F.
As far as possible, the vegetables and drinks are also organic. Fruit juices are 12F a glass, Jade beer 24F. There's a choice of desserts including clafoutis (a type of cherry tart, a Brittany speciality) and tarte au chocolat.
There's another branch of Jardin des Pâtes in the 13th arrondissement.
Also: take-away.

6th arrondissement

Guenmaï

6 rue Cardinale
75006 Paris.
Restaurant. Vegetarian.
Tel: 1-43 26 03 24
In the Latin Quarter, behind the church of St-Germain-des-Prés.
Métro: Saint-Germain-des-Prés or Mabillon

Bus: 48-95-86
Seating 20.
Open: Noon to 3.30pm. Closed Sunday and in August.
Credit cards accepted.
The dining room is bright, very sunny, and the white walls are embell-
ished with green trellis-work. Sophie Daniac opened this macrobiotic
restaurant seventeen years ago with a slogan "We are what we eat."
A Japanese cook, Kimko Saïko, offers you two dishes of the day
(64F) including the famous macrobiotic meal (assiette complète macrobiotique). Also on offer: miso soup (27F), brochettes de seitan (seitan kebabs) with crudités (salad) or légumes (vegetables) (57F),
rouleaux de printemps (spring rolls) (50F).
A fish dish every day.
80% of ingredients are organic and you may quench your thirst with
organic wine (vin bio) 26F a glass or non-organic Bordeaux '82 for
75F a bottle; organic beer, alcoholic (avec alcool) or non-alcoholic
(sans alcool) 19F, fresh fruit juices (jus de fruits frais) 27F, or tea 11F.
Also: take-away, shop, bookshop, talks.

Le Lutétia

Restaurant. Vegetarian-friendly.
23 rue de Sèvres
75006 Paris.
Tel: (La Brasserie) 01 49 54 46 76
Opposite the Bon Marché, and near the organic market in the boulevard Raspail (Sunday morning).
Métro: Sèvres Babylone
Bus: 39-70-83-68-94-84-87
La Brasserie: Open 11.30am to midnight every day, Booking advised.
Credit cards accepted.
The brasserie of the famous Lutétia hotel offers a vegetarian menu at
135F: crême de potiron à la ciboulette (pumpkin soup with chives),
mitonée de chou vert aux châtaignes (green cabbage with chestnuts),
grosses pâtes aux algues et au citron (seaweed and lemon loaf),
pomme reinette au céleri rave (apples with celeriac), riz à la bohémi-
enne (rice), pomme purée (apples), ananas aux poires caramélisées
(pineapple with caramelised pears), glace à la vanille (vanilla ice-
cream), dômede chocolat à la framboise (chocolate dome with rasp-
berries).

The hotel's gastronomic restaurant offers, for 360F, a vegetarian menu called "les saveurs du potager" (the flavours of the kitchen-garden): mêlée de mâche à la truffe et aux noisettes dorées (a blend of lamb's lettuce, truffles and golden hazelnuts), fouillis de légumes, pommes rattes aux châtaignes (mixed vegetables, apples and chestnuts), mêlée de poireaux et de tomates confites, céleri et artichaut à la truffe (a blend of leeks and tomatoes, celery and artichoke with truffles), pressé de chèvre à la sarriette (goat's cheese with savory) and to finish, pointe sablée aux bananes naines, crème légère aux pruneaux (sandy-peak gateau with dwarf bananas, prunes and custard).

Tch'a

Restaurant. Vegetarian-friendly.
6 rue du Pont de Lodi
75006 Paris
Tel: 1-43 29 61 31
Métro: Saint-Michel or Odéon
Bus: 24-21-38-85-96-82-63-87-86-58-70-27
Near the riverside and the Pont-neuf.
Seating 24.
Open: 11am to 7.30pm. Closed on Monday and in August. Booking advised.
This is a traditional Chinese tea-house with a quasi-monastic decor appropriate to meditation which unites the traditional with the modern. The walls are used for exhibitions of Chinese artists. More than 40 kinds of tea, white, yellow, green, red, black etc.(from 20F to 50F). These will be prepared in accordance with unchanging Chinese rituals.
But it is not only a tea-house. You have a choice of four dishes at 73F: two meat, two vegetarian. You may also choose from a vegetarian menu from 100F to 120F: pâté de rave (celeriac pâté) 25F, raviolis pochés maison (ravioli made in house) 25F, champignons parfumés farcis aux légumes (fragrant mushrooms stuffed with vegetables) 46F, tofu gigogne au sésame (sesame tofu) 46F, sauté de noix de cajou, céleri, carrotes, pousses de bambou (stir-fried cashew nuts, celery, carrots and bamboo shoots) 46F, cinq parfums sautés au basilic (five fragrances fried with basil) 46F.
Finally a fine choice of desserts: liserons d'eau (a Chinese water

plant) 27F, gâteaux au thé vert à gelée de thé noir (green tea gateaux with black-tea jelly) 27F, fourré d'ananas à la crême d'abricot (stuffed pineapple with apricot custard) 27F.

7th

La Varangue

Restaurant. Vegetarian-friendly.
27 rue Augerau
75007 Paris.
Tel: 1-47 05 51 22
In the "beaux quartiers", near the Champs du Mars and the Eiffel Tower
Métro: École Militaire
Tel: 42-69-87-80-92-49-28-82
In this traditional restaurant vegetarians will find tarts, flans and vegetables au gratin. A meal (main course + starter or dessert and a glass of cider or wine) costs 77F.

Veggie

Fast-food restaurant. Vegetarian.
38 rue de Verneuil, near the Musée d'Orsay
Tel: 1-42 61 28 61
Métro: Rue de Bac
Bus: 69-68-24-73-83-94-84-63
Vegetarian snack bar in a shop selling natural produce.
Open: noon to 2.30pm Monday to Friday
Veggie offers a choice of soups, salads, hot dishes... you have your platter weighed and are charged accordingly at 99F the kilo. For a complete meal (starter, main course and fresh fruit juice) reckon on about 60F.
Different dishes are offered every day; for example: potimarron au millet (squash with millet), choucroute végétarienne (vegetarian sauerkraut), vegetable pies... The ingredients are organic.
Take-away service in the afternoon.
Also a shop selling organic produce.

8th

La Vie Claire

Fast-food restaurant. Vegetarian.
13 rue de Castellane
Tel: 1-42 65 16 80
Métro: Havre-Caumartin or Madeleine, RER: Auber
Bus: 20-21-22-24-26-27-28-29-32-42-43-52-53-66-80-84-95 (wow!)
Non-smoking, wheelchair access, seating in a corner of a shop selling natural produce.
Open: noon to 2.30pm. Closed Saturday and Sunday. Booking adviced for groups.
Credit cards: CB, Visa and Mastercard accepted.
Good location near the big stores of the boulevard Haussman but not so much a restaurant as a spot where you can have a meal, set in a shop selling organic produce. The shop has a system of ionisation, air purification and aroma diffusion.
Mary-Jane Fredon, dietitian, naturopath and iridologist, offers you three menus (two at 50F, the third at 65F) to eat in or to take away (which is cheaper); for example the 65F menu includes a dish of the day (platter of cereals and proteins with salad or vegetables), a drink, a sesame roll and a dessert of your choice.
Everything served is of course organic and vegetarian. Children generally like the Végétal Burger (veggieburger) and those who want dishes which conform to a particular dietary need have every chance of finding something suitable. Also sandwiches at 25F (vegetable pâté, salad), or 30F (croque-tofu).
Also: take-away, shop selling natural produce, bookshop.

9th

La Fermette d'Olivier

Restaurant. Vegetarian-friendly.
40 rue du Faubourg Montmartre
Tel: 1-47 70 06 88
Behind the Musée Grevin, near the grand boulevards
Métro: Le Peletier or Rue Montmartre

Bus: 74-85-67-20-39-48-42-32-49-43-26
Seating 20
Open: Lunchtime and evening, Monday to Friday.
Credit cards accepted.
A small restaurant at the end of a quiet courtyard in a very busy area.
Meat and fish is served according to the macrobiotic tradition.
Vegetarians will, however, be offered a Zen menu at 70F comprising a
traditional macrobiotic meal (cereals, vegetables and vegetable pro-
teins), a dessert and a drink. The macrobiotic meal by itself costs
50F. The cereals and the wine are organic.

11th

Calypso

Restaurant. Vegetarian.
4 boulevard Jules-Ferry
Tel: 1-43 55 69 09
Near the Place de la République, and not far from the Saint-Martin
canal.
Métro: République or Parmentier
Bus: 96-20-75-65
Seating 25, with outside tables in summer.
Open: noon to 4pm and 7 to 9pm. Closed on Sunday and closed on
public holidays.
Credit cards: Visa
In a modest setting - wooden tables, green plants, white walls and a
large window - Evelyne Dezissert offers a choice of dishes, all with
salad. For example: clafoutis du potager (mixed vegetables pie) 45F,
assiette santé (healthy eating) 45F, gâteau pommes-cannelle (cus-
tard-apple gateau) 20F, au chocolat (with chocolate sauce) 25F.
The bread is made in house from organic ingredients. About 50% of
all ingredients used in the restaurant are organic. For drinks allow 50F
for a bottle of wine or 18F for a glass of fruit juice.
Also: take-away, bookstall, exibition of paintings.

Tenshin

Restaurant. Vegetarian.
8 rue Rochebrune
Tel: 1-47 00 62 44
Near the Mairie (Town Hall) of the 11th arrondissement.
Métro: Voltaire
Bus: 45-56-61-69
Seating 28-38, non-smoking.
Open: noon to 3pm and 7 to 11pm, closed Sunday and August.
Booking advised at weekends.
This restaurant, with a decor and cuisine of Sino-Japanese inspiration, adjoins the natural produce shop "l'Arc en Ciel". There is a set macrobiotic menu at 97F (miso soup with mochi, lettuce, a macrobiotic main course consisting of cereals, vegetables and seitan, followed by the dessert of the day). Or à la carte for between 100F and 150F you will find a choice of macrobiotic dishes: tofu steak, seitan ravioli, five continents salad, soba, udon vegetable fritters (beignets), Japanese gateau.
All ingredients are organic.
The 'assiette macrobiotique' (macrobiotic main course) can be with fish. There is a Côtes-du-Rhône organic wine at 99F.
Also: take-away.

La Ville de Jagannath

Restaurant. Vegetarian.
101 rue Saint-Maur
Tel: 1-43 55 80 81
Between the rue de la République and the rue Oberkampf, before reaching Ménilmontant.
Métro: Saint-Maur Bus: 59-96
Seating 50, one room smoking and one non-smoking, wheelchair access, with outside tables in summer.
Open: noon to 2.30m and 7.30 to 10.30pm (11.30 Friday & Saturday).
Closed on Sunday and Monday lunchtime.
Credit cards: Visa and American Express.
Named after the town of Jagannath, on the east coast of India, which is famous for its temple and the 54 delicious vegetarian dishes which

are offered there every day. This secret culinary art, in the service of
the gods, has been passed down from master to disciple over the mil-
lenia.

Before opening the restaurant in 1996, Tony Armstrong had lived for a
long time in India, where he learnt the art and philosophy of Hindu
vegetarian cookery. He offers a variety of thalis (from 50F to 145F) on
a metal dish with pilau rice, vegetables and (if you wish) dried fruits, a
choice of several dishes such as tomato soup with cumin, iceberg lettuce with pomegranate and grilled almonds (fruits de Grenade et
amandes grillées), des beignets de lentilles croustillants (crispy lentil
fritters).Everything is prepared in-house, even chutney, traditional
breads, fruit or vegetable juices. The decor is in the style of the great
Indian palaces and hotels with the prospect of a veritable gastronomic
experience.

Also: take-away, outside catering, home delivery, cookery courses on
request. Exibition and sale of craft work.

12th

L'Appétit Naturel

Fast-food restaurant. Vegetarian.
8 rue Émilio-Castelar
Tel: 1-43 42 48 90
Near the Place d'Aligre
Métro: Ledru Rollin or Gare de Lyon
Bus: 61-86-76-29-20-65-87-91-24-63-57
Open: 10am to 7pm, closed on Saturday

This little snack-bar is in a shop selling natural produce "L'Appétit
Naturel" (the same proprietor as "Le Grand Appétit"). Here you are
offered tartes aux légumes (vegetable pasties) for 23F, sushi for
10F.... with bières ou jus de fruits (beer or fruit juice) for 14F.
Ingredients are organic and the dishes are prepared following macrobiotic principles. Neither wine, nor meat nor fish is served.

Also: take-away, shop, bookshop.

Cassoulet

13th

La Vie Naturelle

Fast-food restaurant. Vegetarian.
178 avenue Daumesnil
Tel: 1-43 42 34 81
Métro: Daumesnil
A small snack-bar in a shop selling natural produce, for instant
restoration of the inner man or woman.
Tartes aux légumes (vegetable pasties), jus de fruits (fruit juices), jus
de légume (vegetable juices).

Au Jardin des Pâtes

Restaurant. Vegetarian-friendly.
33 boulevard Arago
Tel: 1-45 35 93 67
Métro: Les Gobelins
Bus: 27-83-47-91-21
Open: noon to 2.30pm and 7 to 11pm. Closed Sunday and in August.
Booking advised.
Credit cards accepted.
Same cuisine and menu as the "Jardin des Pâtes" in the 5th
arrondissement, but here Mme Maggio is in charge and the restaurant
is open on Monday.

Le Bol en Bois

Restaurant. Vegetarian.
35 rue Pascal
Tel: 1-47 07 27 24
Near the Manufacture des Gobelins.
Métro: Les Gobelins
Tel: 27-47-83-91
Seating 44, non-smoking.
Open: noon to 2.30pm and 7 to 10pm. Booking advised, especially
Saturday.
Credit cards, Bank and Visa accepted.

The Bol en Bois must be the best known in the capital for vegetarian specialities. It was opened in 1969 with a specifically macrobiotic orientation. Since then the choice has widened but always with organic ingredients.

The midday set meal (64F) includes miso soup, salad, and a plate of cereals, vegetables and seitan tempura.

There is an extensive choice of dishes à la carte including la soupe miso (miso soup) 20F, salade d'algues wakamé (wakame seaweed salad) 35F, tofu frit servi avec des légumes (fried tofu and vegetables) 35F, un bol de riz et pickles servi avec des une soupe miso (a bowl of rice and pickles served with miso soup) 43F.

Desserts: gelée aux amandes (almond jelly), tarte aux pommes (apple pie), crème soja marbrée vanille et chocolat (chocolate and vanilla marbled soya cream), costing 27F to 35F. And to quench your thirst: du vin (wine), de la bière (beer), des jus de fruits (fruit juices), du thé mù (mù-tea), du café de céréales (cereal coffee) or simply de l'eau filtrée (filtered water). Several fish dishes.

Also: take-away. Shop and bookshop in the same street. Cookery courses. Exibitions of paintings.

14th

Aquarius

Restaurant. Vegetarian.
40 rue Gergovie
Tel: 1-45 41 36 88
Not far from the Place de Catalogne and the new area behind the Gare de Montparnasse.
Métro: Pernety or Plaisance
Bus: 48-62-89-95
Seating 50, 3 rooms including one for smokers, wheelchair access.
Open: noon to 2.15pm and 7 to 10.30pm, closed Sunday. Booking advisable Thursday, Friday and Saturday evening.
Credit cards: CB, Amercan Express and Visa accepted
Following the success of the Aquarius in the 4th arondissement this second restaurant was opened in 1980, also as a cooperative.
The chef, Richard Leith, also the author of a recipe book, offers only vegetarian dishes, reputed to be much appreciated also by non-vege-

tarians. He draws his culinary inspiration from all over the world and you will find hummous, chillie sin carne, brownie, apple crumble. For a meal à la carte allow around 85F. The set menu (midday only) is 60F. 60% of the ingredients are organic. On the tables you will find tamari, virgin olive oil, yeast and brown sugar.

The list of beverages includes le quart de vin bio (1/4 organic wine) 18F, la bouteille de bordeaux (a bottle of bordeaux) 65F, jus de fruits frais (fresh fruit juice), bières (beers) and eau minérales (mineral waters).

Also: take-away.

Diététic Shop

Restaurant. Vegetarian.
11 rue Delambre
Tel: 1-43 35 39 75
Métro: Vavin or Edgar-Quinet
Bus: 68-91
Seating 40, non-smoking, outside tables in summer.
Open: 11am to 10.30pm, except Saturday afternoon and Sunday, closed in August.

This restaurant has been in the Montparnasse district for 25 years. The ovens are in the dining room and the macrobiotic inspired dishes are all prepared in front of the customers. 90% of the food comes from the adjoining shop selling natural produce and is therefore organic.

An abundant menu includes specialities such as terrine végétarienne maison (their own vegetable terrine) 30F, la croustillade servie avec les légumes du jour (croustillade with vegetables of the day) 51F, or the "Super-assiette Dietetic shop" consisting of cereals, vegetables and two soya 'boulettes' 51F.

You will also find a choice of plats à base de céréales complètes (wholemeal cereal-based dishes) with vegetables 36F to 46F and all garnished with seaweed. Note also the choucroute et le couscous végétariens (vegetarian sauerkraut and couscous).

Finish off with chocolate dessert 26F, far aux abricots (apricot flan) or far aux pruneaux (dried plum flan) 23F.

And of course a choice of vins bio (organic wines), de thés (teas) and infusions (herbal teas - 11 varieties), des jus de fruits frais (fresh fruit

juices), two amazing cocktails: "le hard", jus de fruits et épices (spicy fruit juices) and "le sweet" made with soya milk.
Also: take-away, shop selling natural produce.

15th

Adi Shakti

Restaurant. Vegetarian.
9 rue Gutenberg
Tel: 1-45 77 90 59
Near the André Citroën park and the Beaugrenelle commercial centre.
Métro: Charles-Michels
Bus: 42-70
Seating 10, non-smoking, wheelchair access.
Open: noon to 14.30 Tuesday to Saturday. Closed in August and during the Christmas holidays. Booking advised.
Credit cards: Visa and Eurocard
Opened in 1986 in a bookshop, Kiran Vyas offers ayurvedic Indian vegetarian cuisine, a complete meal of vegetables, pulses and cereals. Beverages include, of course, thé Indien (Indian tea), tisanes (herb teas), jus de fruits (fruit juices), boissons maison (house beverages) 10F to 15F. The set menu costs 55F, or à la carte reckon on about 80F. 90% of the food including the wine is organic. No meat or fish is served.
Also: take-away, Indian spices for sale, bookshop, cookery courses, yoga, massage, talks.

17th

L'Épicerie Verte

Vegetarian fast food and fish.
5 rue Saussier-Leroy
Tel: 1-47 69 19 68
Near the Place des Ternes and the Arc de Triomphe de l'Étoile
Métro: Ternes
Bus: 30-31-43-92-93

Seating 9, non-smoking.
Open: noon to 7pm, closed on Sunday and in August.
Credit cards: Visa
This little snack-bar in a shop selling natural produce can offer you, naturally enough, organic food. For example: 10 kinds of crudités et de légumes vapeur (salads and steamed vegetables) 16F to 23F, chartreuse de légumes et céréales complètes (mixed vegetables and wholemeal grainss) 43F, flan exotique (exotic flan) 18F, with bread and vin bio (organic wine) or cidre (cider), bière (beer), jus de fruits (fruit juice), eaux minérales (mineral water) 5F to 12F a glass.
Also: take-away, shop selling natural produce, bookshop

Joy in Food

Restaurant. Vegetarian.
2 rue Truffaut
Tel: 1-43 87 96 79
Near Place de Clichy
Métro: Place Clichy or Rome
Bus: 30-54-66-68-74-80-81-95
Seating 16, non-smoking.
Open: noon to 3pm, closed on Sunday. Booking advised. Evening opening for groups is possible.
In this little restaurant Naima Aouad offers you a different dish every day for 43F. Tarte aux épinards et aux pignons (spinach and pine-kernel pie), quinoa aux légumes (quinoa and vegetables), galette de céréales servie avec crudités ou légumes (grain burger served with salad or vegetables). There are also two set menus (58F and 71F) and choice à la carte. 80% of ingredients are organic including the wines, the beers and the sparkling grape juice.
Also: take-away.

18th

Au Grain de Folie

Restaurant. Vegetarian.
24 rue Lavieuville
Tel: 1-42 58 15 57
On the hill, near the Place des Abbesses, in Montmartre.
Métro: Abbesses
Seating 18.
Open: 12.30 to 14.30pm and 19.00 to 22.30 every day. Closed on some public holidays (Christmas, All Saints). Booking advised.
This intimate vegetarian restaurant, 15 years in Montmartre, is one of the 'oldies'. Marie-Cécile Dubois offers you meals à la carte for about 100F; hummus and tzatzikis 25F, guacamole 30F, tarte aux légumes (vegetable pie) 50F, apple crumble 25F, chocolate gateau 35F, a wine list and beer 20F.
Lunchtime and in the evening there are two set menus for 50F and 100F, but the 50F menu is not served after 9.30pm.
The gomasio is prepared in house, and sometimes the bread is baked there too. 50-70% of ingredients are organic.   Vegan dishes are also served (plats végétaliens).
Also: take-away (preferably to order). Cookery courses are envisaged, meanwhile you can buy the restaurant's recipe book, its 'livre de cuisine'.

Rayons de Santé

Restaurant. Vegetarian and fish.
8 place Charles-Dullin
Tel: 1-42 59 64 81
On the hill, opposite the stage-door of the Théatre de l'Atelier, in Montmartre, tucked away in the corner of a square by a hotel.
Métro: Anvers or Abbesses
Bus: 30-54-67-85
Seating 40, smokeless and alcohol free, wheelchair access, tables outside in summer.
Open: noon to 15.00 and 18.30 to 21.30, closed Friday evening and Saturday, and for annual holiday at Easter. Booking advised, espe-

cially for parties or more than four.

Monsieur Varadi has been trying since 1982 to convert the Parisians and artists of Montmartre to vegetarianism, and he has succeeded. He offers pâté végétal (vegetable pâté), terrine de légumes (vegetable terrine), mousse d'artichaut (artichoke mousse), blanquette de champignons (mushrooms in white sauce), galette de tofu (tofu galette) and also dishes inspired by his native Hungary such as seitan goulash, poivrons farcis (stuffed peppers) or roulades de pavots (poppyseed roll).

Allow about 80F for a meal à la carte. There is set menu at 63F or starter + main course for 48F. Beverages: jus de fruit (fruit juice) 15F, la bière sans alcool (alcohol-free beer) 10F, vin sans alcool (alcohol-free wine) 15F le quart (quarter litre), 42F la bouteille (bottle), café de céréales (cereal coffee) 6F. On the table there's bread baked in house, basil, tamari, brewer's yeast and gomasio. 90% of ingredients are organic. There are also vegan, macrobiotic and fish dishes.

Also: take-away, shop (cereals and soya products), bookshop.

19th

La Chouette

Restaurant. Vegetarian-friendly.
113 rue de Crimée
Tel: 1-42 45 60 15
Between the Park des Buttes Chaumont and the Cité des Sciences de la Villette
Métro: Laumière
Bus: 60-75
Open: noon to 14.00 and 19.30 to midnight. Closed Saturday lunchtime and Sunday.
An alternative place promoting local cutlural activities. Vegetarians are catered for in this 'traditional' restaurant with a dish at 49F comprising vegetables and croque-tofu. Really nice salads.

Le Vin

Seine-et-Marne 77

Champeaux

Le Potimarron

Restaurant. Vegetarian.
7 ter, rue de la Libération
77720 Champeaux
Tel: 1-60 66 90 47
South-east of Paris. Leave the A5 motorway at Saint-Germain-Laxis.
Champeaux is on the D215 towards Mormant.
Seats 36. Summer terrace. Parking.
Open Thu-Mon for lunch (not Tue-Wed), also Fri-Sat evening for dinner. Reservations advised on weekends.
Five minutes from the château of Vaux-le-Vicomte, this new restaurant is in an ancient house in a large, bright room opening onto a patio. There is also a second, smaller room with a fireplace and an arched basement. Edwige Piollet has even installed a piano on which she sometimes plays a tune or two, and which she also places at the disposal of customers with budding talent. The cuisine is based on organic produce, either bought in or home-grown. The wholemeal bread is home-baked. There are set menus for 65F at midday and 75F in the evening. Meals à la carte range from 45F to 85F.
Specialities include marrow-based dishes (à base de courges), tofu and kidney bean risotto (risotto au tofu et haricots rouges), cinnamon and orange-zest flavoured ricotta (ricotta à la cannelle), which you can wash down with organic wine (vin bio) at 12.50F a glass or 50F a bottle, or fruit juices (jus de fruits) from 10F to 15F. Fish is served at weekends. For children, options include omelettes, pancakes (crêpes), burgers (galettes). There are also Kousmine diet dishes such as marrow stew (potée à la courge).
Also: take-away, bookshop, concert-dinners.

olive

2. NORTH WEST

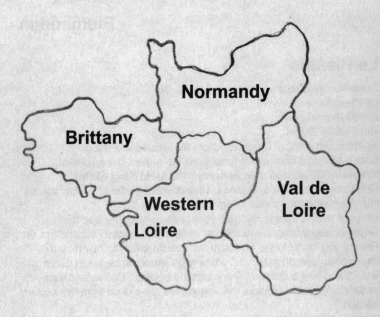

BRITTANY
22 Côtes d'Armor, 29 Finistère, 35 Ille et Vilaine, 56 Morbihan

NORMANDIE
14 Calvados, 27 Eure, 50 Manche, 61 Orne, 76 Seine-Maritime

VAL DE LOIRE
18 Cher, 28 Eure et Loir, 36 Indre, 37 Indre et Loire, 41 Loir et Cher, 45 Loiret

WESTERN LOIRE
44 Loire Atlantique, 49 Maine et Loire, 53 Mayenne, 72 Sarthe, 85 Vendée

Côte-du-Nord 22

Plumaudan

Le Plessis

Guesthouse (board and lodging) Vegetarian
Le Plessis
22350 Plumaudan.
Tel: 2-96 86 00 44
16 km south-west of Dinan. This old farmhouse is a good
setting-off point from which to explore the region: the medieval
fortress at Dinan (ten minutes away), the Mont Saint-Michel,
Combourg, Saint Malo, Rennes. Unless you'd prefer to simply vanish
into the mysterious forest of Arthurian legends.
On your return, Janine Judges, your hostess will offer you a
vegan or vegetarian menu with an impeccable English accent! For 90
Francs you could have, for example: tomato soup, followed by a
mushroom paté on toast and sauce with almonds, beans in garlic, a
leafy salad and a portion of homemade gâteau. Coffee and wine
included. When in season, the vegetables are picked from the kitchen
garden.
Non-vegetarians are catered for by prior arrangement. Le Plessis has
3 guest rooms (125 Francs per night with a hearty breakfast) and a
gîte (from 1900 Francs to 2400 Francs per week according to season).

Saint-Brieuc

Le Millepertuis

Restaurant Vegetarian
Le Millepertuis
4 rue du Gouët
22000 Saint-Brieuc.
Tel. 2 96 33 73 89
Near the covered market (les Halles).
2 rooms, seating for 50. Non smoking restaurant.

Open: 1200-1430 and 1730-2200, Mon-Fri. Possibility of opening on request (by prior arrangement).
Credit cards accepted (Visa). Le Millepertuis is within one of the oldest and most beautiful Breton houses in Saint-Brieuc. There are wooden beams and a superb fireplace inside. Monsieur andMadame Pinabel have thought up various dishes for lunch and dinner for prices ranging from 28 to 120F. You will also find a menu where dishes cost around 90F. House specialities include; seaweed platter, Vitamin platter, vegetable terrine, chiffonade des délices du jardin (ribbons of garden vegetables), home-made tarts, almond cream... accompanied by hop beer, alcohol-free mead, filtered water , home-made organic leavened bread, gomasio and tamari. Vegans, and those on macrbiotic or Kousmine diets will find adapted dishes. 95% of food served is organic. No meat nor fish. This place is 100% veggie, good for vegans, and friendly.
Also: Take-away (cooked dishes or hot dish of the day); health food shop (Saint-Brieuc Nature); book shop; cookery courses; buffet supper once a month on Sunday.

Ille-et-Vilaine 35

Fougères

Samsara

Restaurant Vegetarian-friendly
Samsara
70, rue de la Pinterie
35300 Fougères.
Tel. 2 99 99 68 62
Samsara is a traditional Indian restaurant which had the good idea to offer a vegetarian menu at 85F.

Le vin

Au Saint-Germain-des-Champs

Restaurant Vegetarian-friendly
Au Saint-Germain-des-Champs
12, rue du Vau-Saint-Germain
35000 Rennes.
Tel. 2 99 79 25 52
Opposite the church of Saint-Germain, near the town hall.
35 seats. Disabled access - Summer terrace.
Open from 12 to 2.30pm and from 6.45 to 9.30pm - During the
summer closed on Sundays -
Booking recommended Thursday to Saturday.
Credit cards accepted.
Cook and manager Dominique Fournier opened this restaurant in
October 1994. The ingredients he uses are of biological origin, in particular the vegetables which he selects and buys himself two times a
week in bio-markets. A considerable choice is offered by a menu of
the day (48F), two other menus (59F and 78F at noon, 69F and 88F
in the evening) and a good size à la carte menu (count on about 90F
for a meal à la carte). A few examples: cream of pumpkin soup or
Saint-Germain soup for 22;, warm goat's cheese on toast or crudités
with guacamole and wheat sprouts for 39F; lasagne, couscous, wheat
biscuits or various gratins from 49F to 68F; apple crumble, Joshua
gâteau (with chocolate and almonds) or apple-raisin delight. Or the
gourmand (greedy guts) sweet plate with assorted homemade pastries for 36F. The semi-wholemeal leavened bread is homemade with
filtered water. It is also possible to choose one's tea _ la carte or to
drink cider (39F), wine (67F) or a bio fruit juice. Yeast, gomasio and
shoyu are on the tables. Vegans and those who appreciate macrobiotic cooking will find some appropriate dishes. No meat, but fish is
served. Finally, the kitchen opens onto the first dining-room of the
restaurant, while the other two rooms are brightened up by woodwork
and green plants.
Other activities: take away food, cooking lessons

Scarabée

Restaurant Vegetarian-friendly
Scarabée
57, boulevard Voltaire
35000 Rennes.
Tel. 2 99 30 40 89
Near the Telecom centre.
Bus line no. 7
Dining-hall of 200 m2. 100 seats. Accessible to disabled
persons - Summer terrace - Parking.
Open from 12 to 2pm Mondays to Fridays - Closed in August -
Booking recommended.
Credit cards accepted (Visa, EC).
Jean-François Aubry, Eric Ferchaud and Bruno Jouin have just cele-
brated the 10th anniversary of the opening of their restaurant. Their
cuisine is based on organic products.. They have crudit_s with tahini
sauce, soft pumpkin soufflé, courgette custard tart, vegetarian couscous, tart tatin or carrot cake ... everything washed down with bio
wine (6F for a glass), or beer (13F), or fruit juice (12F) or, simply, with
filtered water freely available. Dishes can be adapted for vegans.
Neither meat nor fish.
Other activities: take away food - Scarabée is also a small
supermarket with biological foods (bio co-op) adjacent to the
restaurant. There's another shop in the nearby suburb of Cesson,
bookshop, cooking lessons.

Thé au Fourneau

Restaurant Vegetarian-friendly
Thé au Fourneau
6, rue du Capitaine Alfred-Dreyfus
35000 Rennes.
Tel. 2 99 78 25 36
Next the Brittany museum, behind the HQ of the newspaper Ouest-
France. 40 seats. Open from 10am to 7pm Mondays to Saturdays.
Credit cards accepted.
In this traditional restaurant, vegetarians can order toasted cheese
sandwiches, vegetable pies: plain (34F) or with crudités (44F).
Other activities: take away food - tea-room in the afternoon.

Loire-et-Cher 41

Azé

La Ferme des Gourmets

Guesthouse (board and lodging) Vegetarian-friendly
Michel and Nadège
Boulay La Ferme des Gourmets
41100 Azé.
Tel. 2 54 80 64 12   Fax: 2 54 72 04 94
3km from the TGV train station of Vendôme. On the D157,
between Le Mans and Vendôme.
At this organic farm, you will be welcomed in an old renovated house,
on the edge of a forest. The farm is classified as having three stars in
the Gîtes de France. It has 3 double and 3 family rooms. The food is
traditional and prepared with organic ingredients grown on the farm.
Specify that you're vegetarian at the time of reservation.
A meal costs 80F. Overnight 210F per person for couples; a week
costs 1200F per person for couples for half board. Single supplement
300F.

Mur-de-Sologne

Domaine de Fondjouan

Restaurant Vegetarian
Domaine de Fondjouan
41230 Mur-de-Sologne.
Tel. 2 54 95 50 00 Fax: 2 54 83 91 77
About 30km from Blois, via the D765 and Cheverny, towards
Vierzon. 10km from Romorantin.
Several dining-rooms (from 40 to 150 m2) - from 30 to 150 seats.
Accessible to disabled persons. Summer terrace - Parking.
Open from 12 to 2.30pm and from 7 to 9.30pm, throughout the
year. Booking advised.
Credit cards accepted (Visa, AE, MC).
In the Sologne countryside, Marie-Claire and André Siméant promise

you peace, silence, a warm welcome and vegetarian catering.
You can eat à la carte (120F to 160F for a meal) or choose a
menu (from 66F to 225F). Some specialities of the house: slimming
green salad with dried fruits (30F), vegetarian couscous (45F), lentils
with tofu (45F), garden pumpkin tart (25F), apple crumble (25F). The
wholemeal bread is of organic origin, just like 20 to 40% of the ingredients, dependent upon the season. On the table you find tamari,
malted yeast, olive oil, water (purified by inverted osmosis) Some of
the wine is organic, just like the prune, orange or grapefruit juice.
The management does its best to serve vegans and fans of
macrobiotic cooking as far as possible and even the die-hard fish
freak or meathead.
Other activities: Hotel, take-away food, bookshop, personal
growth seminars and stress management training courses.

Loire-Atlantique 44

Nantes

L'Arbre de vie

Restaurant Vegetarian
L'Arbre de vie
8, allée des Tanneurs
44000 Nantes.
Tel. 2 40 08 06 10
In the town centre, close to the tower of Bretagne. Look for the
big, scary brasserie Le Carnivore and you will find l'Arbre de Vie just
next to it. Tramstop Morand bridge / 50 otages.
2 dining-rooms, 70 m2. 42 seats. Non-smoking restaurant. Summer
terrace.
Open from 12 to 2pm Tuesday to Saturday, and from 7.30 to 10pm
Thursday to Saturday. Closed in August. Booking advised every day.
Credit cards accepted.
Since 1988 L'Arbre de Vie (The Tree of Life) has been offering vegetarians from Nantes and elsewhere organic dishes from all over the
world, an also themed evenings, cooking courses and take-away
food. Gilles and Christine Daveau have one goal: to surprise people

(even long-standing vegetarians) and to promote a healthy style of cooking which can be very inventive and very elaborate. Gilles, the chef, offers 3 fixed menus (at 64F, 74F and 84F) and an à la carte menu (meals at around 80F at noon, 105F in the evening) based on varied daily specials which reflect provincial, Indian, Moroccan and Mexican gastronomy. He uses wholemeal and bio products such as grains, vegetable proteins, fresh vegetable juice, sprouts and seaweed. He avoids butter and cream and attempts to reconcile gastronomic delight with a synthesis of various healthfood traditions including Kousmine, La Vie Claire and macrobiotics.

Favourite dishes include Tunisian bricks of pear and almonds, accompanied by "harlequin" semolina and Moroccon autumn jardinière, Indonesian tempeh served with rice, vegetable Madras and mushroom kebab fritters, vegetarian sauerkraut with baby vegetables and Muscadet, together with grains and tofu sausages; Quebec tart with pears, nuts and maple syrup. Not forgetting the semi-wholemeal leavened bread, Mont-Roucous water, fresh or bottled fruit or vegetable juice (from 16F to 40F), wine (from 16F to 70F) and, on the table, tamari, yeast, gomasio. Neither meat nor fish.

Other activities: take-away food, cooking courses (10th successful year), dinner debates and shows.

Resto-revues

Restaurant Vegetarian-friendly
Resto-Revues
2, rue du Refuge
44000 Nantes.
Tel. 2 40 47 42 91
Bus 11-12-21-22-23
3 rooms, 43 seats.
Open from 7.30pm to 11pm, Tuesday to Saturday. Closed from 20th July to 20th August. Booking advised for the end of the week.
Credit cards accepted (Visa).
We loved the original review so much that we have done a literal translation. "Once upon a time, a photographer and a cabinetmaker loved each other tenderly. What do you think was the result? From that love came ... a restaurant, well located in the town centre, not far from the cathedral. Thereafter Chantal and Gaëtan have also started to serve meat and poultry ... but they continue to think of us".

On the evening menu (61F) you will find mango and cucumber
salsa, aubergine with cumin terrine, ardéchoise with chapati,
goat's cheese tart with basil, aubergine cake with Roquefort,
courgette and mushroom rolls. The drinks cost around 15F, the wine
is from 40F to 85F.
Other activities: there is a corner where you can read
newspapers and magazines

Orvault

Les Charmes du Forum

Restaurant Vegetarian-friendly
Les Charmes du Forum - Horizon Vert
rue du Commandant Charcot Le Forum
44700 Orvault.
Tel.2 40 94 94 94 Fax: 2 40 06 19 20
Close to Nantes, on the way to Vannes, opposite the Castorama
store. 70 seats. Non-smoking. Parking.
Open from 12 to 2pm, closed on Sunday. Possibly open in the
evening, e.g. for groups if booked. Closed in August.
Credit cards accepted.
This restaurant is on the first floor, on top of the organic self-service
shop Horizon Vert. The food is mixed, but the cook is very keen to
prepare vegetarian dishes and attempts to please everyone. Various
formulas are offered: menu à la carte (28F for a starter, 44F for a
daily special) and multiple menu combination formulas (from 51F to
94F). There is also an organic wine menu (from 51F to 99F for a bottle, 9F for a glass) and a drinks menu, particularly of beers and ciders
(40F a bottle), teas and infusions (herb teas) like Mù tea, tea with
anise aroma, cinnamon, forest fruit or mango tea for 15F.
All products used in the kitchen are of organic origin.
Other activities: Self-service grocer's Horizon Vert: take-away
food, library, cooking courses, occasional entertainment.

La Baguette

Main-et-Loire 49

Fontevraud-l'Abbaye

La Croix Blanche

Restaurant Vegetarian-friendly
La Croix Blanche
49590 Fontevraud-l'Abbaye.
Tel: 2 41 51 71 11 Fax: 2 41 38 15 38
Between Saumur and Chinon, in front of the abbey.
90 seats. Summer terrace with 30 seats. Parking.
Open from 12 to 2.15pm and from 7.30pm to 9.15pm.   Closed 10
days in mid-November and 15 days in January.
Credit cards accepted (V, MC, EC, AE).
Croix-Blance is a classical two-star hotel-restaurant, registered with
"Logis de France", in a setting which goes back to the 12th century,
with 3 fireplaces, a superb summer terrace, stone built with exposed
beams. There is a menu without meat or fish for 99F: a starter with
your choice of crudités, assortment of four vegetables of the day,
choice of cheeses and dessert.
Other activities: crêperie (pancakes), hotel with 21 rooms.

Saint-Georges-des-7-Voies

La Gauvenière

Guesthouse. Vegetarian.
Philippe Vollet La Gauvenière
49350 Saint-Georges-des-7-Voies.
Tel/Fax: 2 41 57 92 75
On the left bank of the Loire, close to Gennes, in between Les
Ponts de Cé and Saumur, on the D751.
Close to Angers, Saumur, Bourgueil and Fontevraud-l'Abbaye, La
Gauvenière is a resting place and a good starting point for exploring
the surrounding treasures of Anjou and Touraine, in particular the
cave-dweller sites dug in the beautiful local white stone. Here you are
offered a single but varied menu which comprises seasonal vegeta-

bles, soya, seitan and tempeh, as far as possible of organic origin.
There are 7 guest rooms with full board for 280F per person, half
board 240F.
Other activities: cooking courses.

Vergonnes

La Blézinière

Guesthouse. Vegetarian.
La Blézinière
49420 Vergonnes.
Tel: 2 41 94 37 23
Halfway between Segré and Châteaubriant.
An English couple, members of the Vegetarian Society (UK), welcome
you to an old farm - at least 200 years old - stone built with wooden
beams and a tiled floor.
The cooking is international (Indian, Italian, English etc) and is
wherever possible based on organic vegetables from the garden and
eggs from the chicken in the back yard. Meals cost 70F. It is
possible to have vegan food on request.
La Blézinière has 2 guest bedrooms (150F with breakfast included)
and 2 gîtes.

Mayenne 53

Renazé

Le Petit Bois Gleu

Guesthouse. Vegetarian.
Le Petit Bois Gleu
53800 Renazé. Tel: 2 43 06 83 86
40km south of Laval, on the N171, via Cossé-le-Vivien and Craon.
Prepare yourself for English style! 5 guest rooms and vegetarian
food! specify this when you make your reservation. It costs 213F per
person half board and 297F per person full board.

Orne 61

Alençon

Au Jardin Gourmand

Restaurant. Vegetarian-friendly.
Au Jardin Gourmand
14, rue de la Sarthe
61000 Alençon.
Tel: 2 33 32 22 56 Fax: 2 33 82 62 60
In the old Saint-Léonard quarter. 25/30 seats.
Open from 12 to 1.30pm and from 8pm to 9.30pm. Closed on Sunday
evening and all day Monday. Open on Sunday evening in summer.
Credit cards accepted.
This traditional restaurant offers a genuinely vegetarian menu for 70F,
put together from, e.g., a chicory salad with nut oil, followed by a 5
grain burger with tapenade (olive paste) and finished by a dessert of
your choice.
Other activities: take-away food, catering.

Ceton

L'Aître

Guesthouse (board and lodging) Vegetarian
L'Aître
Ceton
61260 Le Theil.
Tel: 2 37 29 78 02
About 20km south of Nogent-le-Rotrou.
L'Aître has guest rooms, 250F half board and 320F full board. For
couples 420F and 520F respectively. Vegetarian menu 90F, with wine
included.

Ticheville

La Maison du Vert

Restaurant Vegetarian
La Maison du Vert Le Bourg
61120 Ticheville Vimoutiers.
Tel: 2 33 36 95 84
From Vimoutiers, head for L'Aigle. Ticheville is 6km. In the
village, take the first road on your left towards Pontchardon.
Dining-room with 20 seats. Parking.
Open from 12 to 3pm and from 7.30 to 10pm, closed on Thursday
lunchtime. Closed from 1st to 15th October. Booking necessary in
winter, at least two hours in advance.
Credit cards accepted (CB, V).
In Auge, in Suisse-Normande, Ticheville is a charming, typically
Norman village, with its clock tower, where you can still hear the
angelus, with its ancient priory, its water mill and its vegetarian hotel-
restaurant.
La Maison du Vert was the brainchild of Jill and Colin Kirk who left
London about four years ago for this traditional brick house in the
middle of this beautiful village. In summer they will serve you on the
terrace, in winter by the hearth. The ingredients are 50% organic
and come mostly from their garden.
During the season you can choose between several menus for 50F.
Throughout the year a menu is also served for 110F, noon and
evening, booking needed. The menus change every day. Some
examples: tomato and basil soup, mushroom cone with garden vegetables, fruit crumble and custard. All bread, pastries and jams are
homemade. Vegans are welcome. You can even get meals without
gluten. Neither meat nor fish, of course.
In the hotel, 4 cosy rooms await you, 200F per night, 30F for breakfast.
They also sell some groceries like breads, jams, plants etc.

olive

Vimoutiers

Le Moulin Foulon

Guesthouse. Vegetarian.
Le Moulin Foulon
Aubry-le-Panthou
61120 Vimoutiers.
Tel: 2 33 35 55 46
About 8km along the D979 from Vimoutiers to Gace, at Les Burets
next to a bar, take the turning on the right signposted to Aubry le
Panthou. Take the first right to the village, then the next right again,
before the church, following signs for Le Moulin Foulon.

Pamela Wheatley is the owner/cook of this beautiful Norman house,
once a fuller's mill, lying in a pleasant garden with stream and ponds,

LE MOULIN FOULON
Aubry le Panthou, 61120 Vimoutiers
Normandy

**Specialises in accommodating groups of up to 20 in single, twin
and double rooms. Also two studio rooms 40' x 20'.
Painting, ecology, yoga, reunions. Beautiful surroundings.**

Telephone Pamela 0033-2-33 35 55 46

and extending to 75 acres of land designated as a Nature Reserve.

The particularly inventive vegetarian menu has an international tendency derived from Pamela's extensive travels and includes items from the Far and Middle East, as well as European cuisines.
Everything is home-made including the bread, jam, chutneys, more than 50% of the ingredients are organic, and during the season come from the kitchen garden and orchard. All water is from the spring. No fish or meat is served.
The evening meal is five courses served with wine or local cider. A range of herbal teas is available as well as normal teas and coffee. Special dietary requirements understood and catered for.

Bedrooms are in the main house or annexes, and there are two large activity rooms. Le Moulin Foulon is an ideal place for a Retreat, or for courses which in the past have included yoga, ecology, personal development, drama, and writing. Individual guests are also welcomed when possible. Cost - F250 half board per person.

Sarthe 72

Le Mans

Vita-Mine

Restaurant Vegetarian Vita-Mine
5 rue Auvray 72000
Le Mans. Tel: 2 43 28 67 15
In town centre. Non-smoking restaurant.
Open: Tuesday through Friday noon to 2pm.
Credit cards accepted: Visa.
Vita-Mine offers a simple vegetarian cooked menu, with organically grown produce. Every day five specials such as pies and vegetable bakes, within a 26F to 32F price range. Organic wine 35F the bottle. No meat, no fish.

Seine-Maritime 76

Dieppe

Ankara

Restaurant. Vegetarian-friendly.
Ankara
18-20 rue de la Rade
76200 Dieppe
Tel: 2 35 84 58 33
In the Bout du Quai district, near the marina.
Seating 70. Disabled access.
Open: noon to 2pm and 7 to 10pm. Closed on Wednesday. Booking
advised at the week-end. Credit cards: Mastercard and Visa.
This restaurant, pleasantly decorated in an oriental style,
offers a set vegetarian menu at 80F. A la carte you will find, in addi-
tion to traditional Turkish dishes, some oriental vegetarian ones, a
vegetarian "mezze": aubergines farcies (stuffed aubergines), poivrons
farcis (stuffed peppers) with bulgar-wheat, as well as famous Eastern
pastries. For a meal à la carte reckon on about 120F, and wines at
about 80F.
Also: take-away, bookshop with essentially books about Turkey, a
play corner and reading matter for children.

Le Havre

Le Taj Mahal

Restaurant. Vegetarian-friendly.
Le Taj Mahal
98 rue Saint-Jacques
76600 Le Havre Tel: 2 35 21 56 02
Closed Saturdays and Sunday lunchtime.
This Indo-Pakistani restaurant serves several dishes which contain
neither meat nor fish including dhal (lentilles indiennes) and aubergine
fritters (beignets d'aubergines). Even the set menu at 99F has suffi-
cient vegetarian dishes to fill you up.

Rouen

Gourmand' Grain

Restaurant. Vegetarian.
Gourmand' Grain
3 rue du Petit Salut
76000 Rouen
Tel / Fax 02 35 98 15 74
Near the cathedral. Open: 12.00-14.00 Tuesday-Saturday.
The only vegetarian restaurent in Seine-Maritime, in the heart of the pedestrian area of Rouen. They are next to a shop called Natural which sells, you've guessed it, natural produce and hence the restaurant uses only quality ingredients. The dish of the dayat 44F always includes salad. Set menus are 42F and 65F. Specialities include couscous, moussaka or broccoli gratin. A la carte, there are always burgers (galettes) and tarts (tartes) from 35F to 45F, desserts at about 19F and organic red wine from Gard (vin bio rouge du Gard) at 14F a glass. The chef tries to follow the dietary principles of Dr Kousmine. Oil is from the first pressing, water is filtered and a glass of herb tea is offered free with each meal.
Also: shop selling natural produce.

The Hitch-hiker's Guide to the South of France

Back in the days before I could afford hotels, I used to spend student vacations travelling around France with a union jack and a stiff thumb. In 1993 I took a year off to write and so, to save money, I dusted off my old skills travelling around the south and then from Cannes to Calais with my Kiwi companion Kerry.

Contrary to what it said in the *Hitch-hiker's Guide to Europe*, I'd always found hitching in France easy. Roads are long and there are plenty of bored drivers glad of the chance to help improve your French. Hitch slow moving traffic with a long pull in, off roundabouts or at the péages (motorway toll booths). By myself or with Kerry I found it could take anything from a few minutes to two hours. Kerry alone averaged about five minutes. We used a giant marker and cardboard sign with svp (s'il vous plaît).

Cagnes-sur-Mer is one long beach with heaps of camp sites, a bus or boat ride from St Tropez, but one twentieth the cost. We pitched our two person tent for 20F a night - there's always room for a little one. It's just one cheap oasis in a glorious coastline of beautiful coves and long, sandy beaches that we visited from Marseille to the Italian border and beyond. Camping in youth hostel grounds is half the price of inside but you can use all the facilities, and they are in cheaper areas close to the expensive places. From the supermarket we bought all the goodies we'd eat in Britain plus Mediterranean delicacies.

We started each day with a swim in the Mediterranean, breakfasted on warm baguettes and fruit, lounged on the beach, chatted and wrote and read and had the most wonderful summer ever walking hand in hand in the place of our dreams.

In September many head inland for the grape harvest. But that's another story....

Safety tips: When offered a ride, ask the driver where they're going. If you don't like their demeanour, pretend to be a dumb tourist going the other way. Don't get in a car with two or more guys. A wallet with a day's cash is expendable, as is a money belt stuffed with easily replaced travellers cheques. I've never once felt myself to be threatened or in danger. However it is sensible to travel in pairs which I usually do myself, even though I have a brown belt in karate.

3. NORTH EAST

NORD/PAS DE CALAIS
59 Nord, 62 Pas de Calais

PICARDY
02 Aisne, 60 Oise, 80 Somme

ALSACE: 67 Bas-Rhin, 68 Haute-Rhin

BURGUNDY: 21 Côte d'Or, 58 Nièvre, 71 Saône et Loire, 89 Yonne

CHAMPAGNE-ARDENNE: 08 Ardennes, 10 Aube, 51 Marne, 52 Haute Marne

FRANCE-COMTÉ: 25 Doubs, 39 Jura, 70 Haute-Saône, 90 Belfort

LORRAINE-VOSGES: 54 Meurthe et Moselle, 55 Meuse, 57 Moselle, 88 Vosges

Ain 01

Saint-Etienne-sur-Reyssouze

Le Vert Bocage

Guesthouse Vegetarian-friendly
Georges and Ariette Chervet
Le Vert Bocage
Hameau de Cornans
01190 St. Etienne-Sur-Reyssouze
Tel/Fax: 03-85 30 97 27
On the N6, between Tournus and Macon, at Fleurville, head east till
Pont-de-Vaux then take the D26 as far as
Saint-Etienne-sur-Reyssouze. In the village turn right for
Boissey. Vegetarian meal, if requested at time of booking. In
the heart of the Bresse countryside you will find this peaceful
place with lots of flowers and a pretty little pond, Le Vert
Bocage (The Green Grove), rated three stars in the G_tes de
France. Georges and Arlette Chervet will welcome you to their
Bressan farm, which has five separate bedrooms, each with an en
suite bathroom/shower. Bed and breakfast is 200F single but only
220F (total) if there are two of you! For more than one night the price
drops to 175F for one person, and 190F for two. There is an evening
meal for around 70F, but please note it isn't automatically vegetarian
so any requests for a vegetarian meal must be made at the time of
booking. Fresh homemade Borsa bread is served at the table, and
produce used for cooking is 90% organic, which you can also find on
sale at the farm.

Côte-d'Or 21

Dijon

Le Potimarron

Restaurant. Vegetarian.
Le Potimarron
4 avenue de l'Ouche
21000 Dijon.
Tel: 3 80 43 38 07
Near to a canal, in the port area of town, opposite the ambulance station. Non-smoking restaurant with space for 30. Terrace available in summer with room for 12.
Closed all day Sundays, Mondays; also closed Wednesday evenings (group reservations excepted). Credit cards accepted.
A menu at 80 Francs has a selection including: vegan sauerkraut (choucroute végetal), oven-baked buckwheat crêpes (crêpe au sarraisn fourée), vegan paté, soya croquettes and the house speciality fromagets - prepared with fresh goat's cheese. The produce is on the whole organic and will appeal to both macrobiotic palates and carnivores.
Other facilities: take-away, wholefood shop, bookshop, deli (not entirely veggie).

La Vie Saine

Restaurant. Vegetarian.
La Vie Saine
29 rue Musette
21000 Dijon.
Tel: 3 80 30 15 10
Open only for lunch Monday to Saturday. Unfortunately there is not much information on this vegetarian restaurant. The dish of the day costs 45 Francs. Ingredients are most probably organic as La Vie Saine is also a wholefood shop. Fish is also served.

Doubs 25

Besançon

La Récréation

Restaurant. Vegetarian-friendly.
La Récréation
12, rue Luc-Breton
25000 Besançon.
Tel: 3 81 83 00 03
In the city centre, between the pedestrianised road and the
market place.
Bus: Place Saint-Pierre station (towards the town centre).
Seats 25. Summer terrace. Open: from 07.00 for breakfast, 11.30 for
lunch and 18.30 for dinner. Closed Sunday. Reservations advisable
in summer. Credit cards accepted.
The restaurant is a small room with a verandah for winter and
a superb terrace in summer. Sylvie Philipona welcomes a mainly
female clientele, vegetarian and not. For those who are
vegetarian, there are specific dishes such as soya steak and
ratatouille (45F), émincé de poireaux au tofu (leek ribbons with
tofu for 45F), vegetarian salads (40F), l'épinard au chèvre
chaud (spinach with warm goat's cheese for 45F), galettes de
pommes de terre au fromage (potatoe pancakes with cheese for
40F). Also: Take-away.

Marne 51

Reims

Le Taj Mahal

Restaurant. Vegetarian-friendly.
Le Taj Mahal
151, rue de Vesle
51100 Reims

Tel: 3 26 40 03 50
Open every day.
The à la carte menu of this Indian restaurant contains numerous
starters (about 22F) and mains (from 40 to 45F) without meat or fish.
The fixed menu, for 95F, has enough dishes for vegetarians to be
easily satisfied.

Nord 59

Lille

La Source

Restaurant. Mostly vegetarian.
La Source
13, rue du Plat
59800 Lille. Tel: 3 20 57 53 07. Fax: 03 20 54 65 69.
Close to the station (Flandre). Station République/Ribour.
130 seats. Disabled access. Non-smoking restaurant. Summer terrace.
Open every day (except Sunday) from 11.30 am to 1.30pm and
Friday evening from 7pm to 9pm. Closed during the first three weeks
of August.   Booking advised. Credit cards accepted (Visa).
Denis Penez (not to be confused with Dennis Pennis) founded this
restaurant 18 years ago and he continues to manage it with lots of
enthusiasm. A vast, bright dining-hall with a sheltered terrace make
this a convivial place which is well known by the the Lillois. The
restaurant is adjacent to a health food shop of the same name. The
chef offers a vegetarian hot dish for 48F every day with either a grain
or soya dish, accompanied by 4 vegetables and a pulse, or a large
salad with dressing. You can also opt for one of the menus (44F -
55F - 67F - 75F). There are also desserts à la carte: tarte maison
17F, soja cream 17F, chocolate mousse 19F. Wine is 65F for a bottle,
or sup fruit juices, tea or coffee substitutes such as Pagode tea and
Yannoh. The ingredients are bio and you can sprinkle on typical vegetarian seasonings such as beer yeast, gomasio, salt with herbs and
wheatgerm. There are also a daily fish dish and one poultry dish.
Other activities: take-away food, health food shop

Pas-de-Calais 62

Boulogne-sur-mer

Chez Alfred

Restaurant. Vegetarian-friendly.
Chez Alfred
24, place Dalton
62200 Boulogne-sur-Mer
Tel: 3 21 31 53 16. Fax: 3 21 33 86 21.
In the town centre, opposite the Saint-Nicolas church.
38 seats. Disabled access. Summer terrace with 50 seats.
Open continuously from 11am to 10pm. Closed from 22nd December
to 22 January. Booking advised on Saturday and bank holidays.
Credit cards accepted.
In this traditional restaurant, specialising in seafood, vegetarians can
get a specially prepared dish for 45For go for other dishes on the
menu such as soups, salads, pasta, pizzas. Wines start at 69F.
Also: take-away.

Bas Rhin 67

Hagenau

Cassegraine

Restaurant. Vegetarian.
Cassegraine
7, rue du Rempart
67500 Hagenau
Tel: 3 88 73 91 05
Close to the station.
Self-service. 50 seats. Non-smoking restaurant.
Open from 11.45am to 2pm Monday to Friday.
This self-service restaurant is run by the Association Graine
(Groupement Alternatif d'INitiatives Écologiques) whose aim is

"the promotion of cultural activities, leisure and others, to assure the protection of living beings against all polutions, physical as well as psychical ...." It is open to everyone. Every day there are at least 2 plats du jour (daily specials) for 40F, one vegetarian, the other traditional (with meat), and 7 small dishes starting from 18F. The plats du jour are accompanied by crudités or by soup. The ingredients are essentially organic. You can quench your thirst with sparkling mineral water (7F), bio wine (42.50F for a bottle, 15F a quarter litre), alcohol-free beer (10F) or cereal beer (13F), cider (9F), fruit juice (8F) or teas, tisanes (herb teas) and coffee (5F).

The à la carte menu has a macrobiotic dish for 35.50F. Lastly, and this is something that's so rare in France it deserves special praise, there is a daily vegetarian dish specifically for children for 28F.

Other activities: take-away food, cooking courses, organic market on Friday from 4.30pm to 7.30pm, meetings and courses on health, ecology and solidarity.

Strasbourg

A.D.A.N.

Restaurant. Vegetarian.
6, rue de Sédillot
67000 Strasbourg
Tel: 3 88 35 70 84
Tram station Étoile.

50 seats. Disabled access. Non-smoking restaurant. Summer terrace. Open from 12am to 2pm, Monday to Saturday. Open Friday evening, from 7pm to 10pm, only after booking. Closed in August.

A.D.A.N. stands for Association pour le Développement de l'Alimentation Naturelle (Association for the Development of Natural Foods). This is their vegetarian, organic restaurant. It is open to everyone and is organised on a partly self-service basis, where you collect your food at the counter, which does result in swifter service than in other restaurants. There are three menus for 56F (51F for the members of the Association), plus another menu ranging from 38F up to 70F. A special menu for 90F is served on the last Friday of the month in the evening.

Among the side dishes are vegetable paté (17F), tofu or

seitan kebab (25F), shepherd's pie made with soya, seitan stew, lentil bread with nuts, vegetarian sauerkraut. For dessert there is "bonne-mine" (good looks) cake, apple and rosemary cake, or pavé cake without sugar but "with seven flavours". All this is accompanied by organic bread and you can choose from the wine list, fruit juice, cereal beer (bière à l'épeautre). There is always a macrobiotic dish and others that are egg and dairy-free. No meat or fish.
Other activities: take-away food, catering service, cooking courses, lectures on ecology and natural medicines, painting exhibitions.

Poëles de Carottes

Restaurant. Vegetarian.
Poëles de Carottes
18, rue de la Krutenau
67000 Strasbourg
Tel: 3 88 35 74 74. Fax: 3 88 44 07 22.
The street is on the corner of the Saint-Guillaume church, in the Krutenau quarter, and the restaurant is opposite the tobacco factory. 25 seats. Summer terrace. Parking.
Open from 12 to 2.30pm and from 7pm to 10.30pm. Closed on Sunday. Closed in August. Booking advised.
Credit cards accepted.
Just two years old, Poëles de Carottes takes care over its modern and stylish decor, with frescos painted on the walls.
Everyone working here are themselves vegetarian and they offer a varied and aromatic cuisine. Eating à la carte costs 39F to 120F. There is a single setmenu at noon (45F) and three in the evening (69F, 84F, 99F). You can have things like avocado paté on home-made bread, vegetarian burger, pizza or soufflé. All desserts are home-made, such as fruit tarts and tiramisu. The ingredients are about 60% organic. No meat or fish. Vegans can be adapted for.
Other service: take-away food.

cassoulet

Haut Rhin 68

Mulhouse

Le Maharajah

Restaurant. Vegetarian-friendly.
Le Maharajah
8, rue des Tanneurs
68100 Mulhouse
Tel: 3 89 56 48 21
Closed Monday lunchtime.
This Indian restaurant offers a special vegetarian à la carte
menu with starters from 27F to 30F and main courses 60-67F.

La Tête de Chou

Restaurant. Vegetarian.
La Tête de Chou
14, rue des Trois Rois
68100 Mulhouse
Tel: 3 89 46 22 17
In the town centre. 40 seats.
Closed Saturday evening, all day Sunday, Monday evening.
Credit cards accepted.
La Tête de Chou (Cabbage Head) offers a menu for 55F every mid-
day. A la carte you will discover vegetable turnover with ginger (64F),
pie with vegetable paté (53F), etc. The ingredients are organic as far
as possible and so are the drinks, such as Bordeaux wine.

Haute Saône 70

Fouvent

La Pierre Percée

Guesthouse. Vegetarian.
Anne Kringhs
Domaine de la Pierre Percée
70600 Fouvent
Tel: 3 84 31 30 46
On the N19, midway between Langres and Vesoul, at Cintrey, head
for Morey, Seaucourt, then turn right for Fouvent-le-Bas.
In an old farmhouse dating back to 1830, of white stone with a tiled
roof, and beans and panelling in solid oak. The farm is isolated, in
the middle of a deciduous forest which is a nature reserve, an excellent starting point for discovering on foot or horseback the menhirs,
ponds, medicinal springs and other interesting places. The menu is
vegetarian the meals vary in price between 50F and 100F. Anne
Kringhs prepares especially seitan, tofu, brown rice and organic fruits
and vegetables from her garden. The wholemeal leavened bread is
homemade. All the ingredients are organic, including the wine and
fruit juices, or you can enjoy the medicinal spring water. Vegans and
macrobiotic enthusiasts can easily obtain appropriate dishes. Meat
and fish are only served by special request. No problem if you speak
German, English or Dutch. Anne Kringhs, her daughter and son can
answer in all of these languages. You'll pay about 100F per night,
breakfast included.
Other activities: cooking and yoga courses, retreats.

Saône-et-Loire 71

Chalon-sur-Saône

La Pierre Vive

Restaurant. Vegetarian.
7, rue de Strasbourg
71100 Chalon-sur-Saône.
Tel: 3 85 93 39 01
On the Ile Saint-Laurent. Seating 60. Disabled access. Non-smoking
restaurant. Summer terrace in June and July. Parking.
Open 11.00h to 15.00h, except Sunday and Monday. Closed August.
Reservation advised for groups.
Monsieur Buisse, who is both the cook and manager in this
restaurant with walls of brick and stone and exposed timber
beams, has 12 years experience of vegetarian cuisine. There is a
58F menu where you pick your choice from a buffet of starters and
hot dishes. Desserts and pastries are 8F and there is also home
made wholemeal bread. Wines 40-60F plus other drinks such as
herb tea, teas and coffee. Vegans and those following the Montignac
diet can also be catered for. No meat nor fish.
Also: take-away, exhibitions, training.

Somme 80

Amiens

La Soupe à Cailloux

Restaurant. Vegetarian.
16 rue des Bondes
80000 Amiens. Tel: 3 22 91 92 70.
In the Saint-Leu district, near the cathedral. Seats 45. Summer
terrace. Open: 12.00-14.00 and 19.00-23.00. Closed on Monday (but
open every day in summer). Closed from Christmas to New Year.
Credit cards: EC, MC, AE

Originally an exclusively vegetarian restaurant when it opened
18 years ago, the manageress Collette Bultez now offers a mixed cuisine based where possible on organic ingredients.
The set menus are 67F (lunchtime only) and 95F. An à la carte meal
costs from 100F to 130F, and wine is from 60F to 140F. In a room
with warm colours and an Italian style decor, vegetarians will find
dishes including vegetables au gratin (gratins de légumes), burgers
(galettes de céréales), pastries with nuts or hazelnuts (gâteaux aux
noix, gâteaux aux noisettes).

Belfort 90

Belfourt

La Conviviale

Restaurant. Vegetarian.
La Conviviale
18 rue de Brasse
90000 Belfort
Tel 3-84 28 28 06
Near the bank Caisse d'Epargne
50 seats. Disabled access. Summer terrace.
Open: 12.00-13.30, closed Sunday and in August. Reservations recommended.
This restaurant is managed by a charity and has been going for 17
years. It occupies three small rooms in a nineteenth centuryhouse
and offers a set menu at 50F, as well as dishes à la carte from 30F to
74F. Dishes include houmous, salade complète, lasagne, vegetable
pasties with morbier cheese (tartes de légumes au morbiers), various
souffles (soufflés divers), raspberry charlottes (charlottes aux framboise). Wine is 36F a bottle, apple juice (jus de pommes) 5F a glass,
local beer (bière ch'ti) 9F. Bread is wholemeal and organic, as are
80% of the ingredients used. Yeast, gomsio and shoyu are on the
tables. For children, there are burgers (galettes de céréales). The
positively eclectic nature of the society enables it to respond to any
dietary need, except of course the provision of meat or fish.
Also: take-away.

4. SOUTH EAST

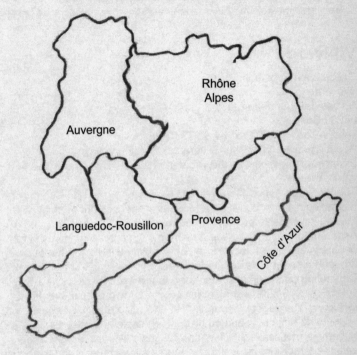

AUVERGNE: 03 Allier, 15 Cantal, 43 Haute-Loire, 63 Puy de Dôme

COTE D'AZUR: 06 Alpes-Maritimes, 83 Var

LANGUEDOC-ROUSILLON
11 Aude, 30 Gard, 34 Hérault, 48 Lozère, 66 Pyrénées-Orientales

PROVENCE: 04 Alpes de Haute-Provence, 05 Hautes-Alpes
13 Bouches du Rhône, 84 Vaucluse

RHONE ALPES: 01 Ain, 07 Ardèche, 26 Drôme, 38 Isère
42 Loire, 69 Rhône, 73 Savoie, 74 Haute-Savoie

Alpes-de Haute-Provence 04

Cruis

Vitaverde

Guesthouse Vegetarian
Vitaverde
Au Jas de Boureti-Le Claus
04230 Cruis
Tel: 04-92 77 00 89 Fax: 04-92 77 02 33
About 25km south west of Sisteron. Self-catering flats.
Reservation essential as the vegetarian supper is served only 2 or 3
times a week.
The Vitaverde Association was first established in a 17th Century
house, built at the foot of Lure Mountain, east of Mont Ventoux in
Haute Provence, to promote green and cultural tourism. The
Association runs 5 three-star country gîtes, each accommodating 2-5
people in two bedrooms, with an old-fashioned living room with open
fire, and a buffet-style vegetarian meal on offer 2 or 3 times a week.
Depending on the time of year, for a four person flat you pay 1,715 to
2,435F, or 205-300F per night for a room for two people, breakfast
included. The vegetarian meal, 110F including drinks, is organic. You
might have have la soupe au pistou (vegetable and basil soup),
aubergine moussaka, chick peas with goats' cheese, apricot and
sesame tart or almond ice cream, with leavened bread and the house
liqueur. Fruits and vegetables are picked from the organic garden and
orchard, which you will also find on sale, together with fruit juice and
honey. They don't use meat or fish. Vegan meals may be requested
at the time of booking. Activities include talks and conferences on
vegetarianism and veganism and rambling while fasting.

Digne-les-Bains

Villa Gaia

Pension Vegetarian
Villa Gaia
Route de Nice
04000 Digne-Les-Bains
Tel: 4- 92 31 21 60 Fax: 4-92 31 20 12
On Route Napoleon Capacity for 20 guests. Easy access for
disabled persons.
Summer terrace and car park.
Open every day 12.30-20.00. Reservations essential.   Closed 15
November - 15 March.
Credit cards welcome.
This family mansion nestles in the middle of a beautiful
property, which is covered with trees some over a hundred years old.
The owners, who are vegetarian, offer you a single set menu at 150F
for lunch and 175F in the evening, with soup, salads, home made
fresh pasta, pies, pastries, sorbets, crumbles etc, all served with fresh
organic bread, Guérande unrefined salt and gomasio. The kitchen
garden and Victorian glasshouse provide thebulk of the ingredients,
75% of them organic. Organic wine is 75F a bottle, tea or herb tea
from the garden 15F. Villa Gaia is also a hotel. They also sell jam and
have cookery courses held on request for groups of 10.

Greoux-les-Bains

La Maison Verte

Guesthouse Vegetarian
La Maison Verte
7 Vallon Paradis
04800 Greoux-Les-Bains
Tel: 04-92 74 21 20
50km north of Aix-en-Provence or 15km east of Manosque. When
you reach Greoux-les-Bains, at the Gryselis roundabout, turn off
towards Valensole. In July and August, evening meal only; the rest of
the year, lunch only. Closed Wednesdays.   Credit cards welcome.

Greoux-les-Bains has been famous since ancient times
for its thermal spa for healing asthma, other respiratory
problems and rheumatism. There are also excursions to the
lavender fields of the Valensole plateau, Verdon canyons and
Lake Esparron. La Maison Verte (The Green House) welcomes you
for holidays or a course of treatment. The bedrooms or studios
accommodate 2-4 people. Allow on average 230F per person per day.
La Maison Verte is also a table d'hôte. You can dine in a large, shaded garden, near the kitchen garden which provides the food for the
table, 80% of which is organic. Jacqueline Feldman,landlady and
chef, was formerly the owner (1980-94) of the vegetarian restaurant
La Table Verte (The Green Table). At La Maison Verte, she offers you
one menu per sitting, consisting of one or two choices for 74F including for example olive crust pie, seaweed salad, seitan or tofu dishes,
various fruit tarts such as quince, seaweed custard tart, walnut cake
etc with (organic or normal) wine 35F per bottle, local apéritifs 10F,
fruit and veg juice cocktails.

Sigonce

Chante l'Oiseau

Guesthouse & nature centre Vegetarian-friendly
Chante L'Oiseau,
04300 Sigonce
Tel: 04-92 75 24 35
95km west of Avignon, by the N100 via the town of Apt. From
Forcalquier, carry on to Sigonce, and the Chante L'Oiseau
(Singing Bird) nature centre is situated 500m away in the hills,
after the church.
Closed certain days during mid November and mid January.
In the Haute-Provence (High Provence) of Forcalquier lies a
private and peaceful little hamlet with self-catering gîtes and
the main house accommodating 20 guests. Jean-Claude and
Nathalie Genin, the hosts of Chante L'Oiseau, welcome their
guests into their provençale home, offering both lunch and
dinner options for 75 francs a head. There are a range of different
dishes, according to the time of year, and a good percentage of the
ingredients are freshly picked from the house's garden and orchard.

You may choose the onion and red wine pie with the goat's cheese seven leaf salad, creamy tomato and pumpkin soup, or the mushroom vol au vonts, followed by a choice of desserts, like strawberry souffle or red berry mousse, all accompanied by home made bread. Vegans will easily find something tasty. Your hosts offer a house aperitif (10 francs) to wet your appetite, and have various other drinks, such as thyme wine (40 francs), herb teas (7 francs) and other home made juices. Do not hesitate to ask for directions for nice rambles. With a bit of luck, the manager will go with you and give you a free lesson in provencale ornithology. There is also a bookshop and a meeting room for groups and seminars

Hautes-Alpes 05

Névache

La Joie de Vivre

Ferme-Auberge (Farm-Inn) Vegetarian-friendly
La Joie de Vivre
Hameau de Sale
05100 Nevache
Tel: 4 92 21 30 96 Fax: 4 92 20 06 41
After reaching Briançon, take the road towards
Italie-Montgenevre, then turn left towards Nevache.
Large dining room seating 30 people. Patio and car park.
Table d'hote open to non-residents.
Reservation required during French school holiday periods.
Credit cards: Visa
This Farm House has two specialities: dishes which are
traditional to the Alps and vegetarian cuisine, the latter
offering you the choice between two set meals at 85 and 130
francs, or an a la carte menu ranging from 120 to 170 francs.
Ingredients are 60% organic, including the bread, wine and beer.
They offer omelette 37F, mushroom fondue 85F, red berry gratin 24F,
pear and almond tart 20F... accompanied by a local wine (35cl - 35F)
or a Jade Beer for 24F.
You might decide to hire out the Social Room for the evening,

where you and your friends can listen to jazz and talk the night
away in front of an open fire. For 20 years Joie de Vivre (Joy
of Living) has been a resort at 1600m, in the peaceful alpine
hamlet of Sale. Several special breaks are offered in
three-star rooms such as the Escapade deal from Friday night to
Sunday afternoon, with full board for two people costing 970F. Allow
225F per person per day for half board.

There's also a bookshop which has newspapers and books on the
mountains, trips with llamas, and in the property's grocery
store, "L'Epicerie de Claire" you can buy fruit, vegetables, and
home- made take-away dishes and desserts.

Alpes-Maritimes 06

Cannes

Chez Max

Restaurant Vegetarian-friendly
Chez Max
11, rue Louis-Perrissol
06400 Cannes.
Tel: 4 93 39 97 06
In the Suquet quarter, near the musée de la Castre.
Open 12.00 to 14.00 and 19.00 to 22.00.   Closed Mondays.
Disabled access. Summer terrace.
In her traditional tavern, Madame Gassmann will offer you a
genuine vegetarian (but not vegan) menu for 85F, featuring Max salad
or gratin of vegetables followed by home-made fresh pasta and
cheese or dessert of the day.
The emphasis is on pasta, which are freshly home-made with
different sauces: pesto à la Genovese, crème champignons (cream of
mushroom), Roquefort, raviolis aux épinards (spinach ravioli). Also
Swiss fondues.

olive

Guillaumes

Le Trauc

Guesthouse Vegetarian-friendly Ferme-auberge
Le Trauc Bantes
06470 Guillaumes.
Tel/Fax: 4 93 05 54 64
Approximately 100km north of Nice, taking the N202 and then the
D2205. At Saint-Sauveur-sur-Tinée, take a left towards Beuil, Valberg
and Guillaumes. The farm is 13km north of this village.
Closed November-March.
Beate and Ingo Lagenbach are farmers in the Haut-Var mountains.
The farm, with its old buildings, is isolated, 1300m up on a south-fac-
ing slope with a gorgeous view. The farmhouse meals are prepared
using traditional farm products including cold meats and very unlucky
home-reared meat. If you're still
reading, Beate does think of vegetarians and can offer a menu at
140F (90F for guests) with crudités (salad), raviolis aux 3
fromages (3 cheese ravioli), gratins, tartes aux légumes
(vegetable tart), escalopes au millet (millet escalopes),
home-made pastries, all washed down with organic wine at 50F.
Also: guest accommodation (3 apartments for 4-6 people); farm produce for sale; cookery courses on request.

Nice

Noori's

Restaurant Vegetarian-friendly
Noori's
1 Place Garibaldi
06000 Nice.
Tel: 4 93 82 28 33
Open every day. Reservations recommended at weekends.
This Indian restaurant has a good selection of vegetarian dishes
including vegetable curry 49F, vegetable biryani and cheese
samosas. On Sundays there is a help-yourself buffet which
includes 6 or 7 vegetarian dishes for 99F per person.

Tourne-sol

Restaurant Vegetarian
Tourne-sol
57 avenue Cyril-Besset
06100 Nice.
Tel/Fax: 4 93 52 67 32
Opposite the Saint-Barthélémy post office.
Bus 5, 7, 4, 26.
Seats 15.
Open: from 12.00 Tues-Sat. Reservations advisable.
Credit cards accepted, minimum charge 300F.
Tourne-sol was founded by a couple who have been working
together for 8 years. Organic caterers to start with, 5 years
ago they decided to open this calm, intimate, homely restaurant
where a fixed menu costs 80F and à la carte ranges from 50-100F.
Accompanied by bread made with organic yeast and filtered water
you could order, for example, une tarte or une quiche aux legumes for
30F (vegetable tart or quiche), a chili d'azukis (aduki bean chilli), pain
de maïs avec endives aux champignons for 55F (corn bread with
endives and mushrooms). For dessert try gâteau au chocolat (chocolate cake), bavarois (fruit mousse) and granola for 30F. All washed
down with jus de fruits (fruit juice), organic beer for 15F and vin de
Bourgogne (Burgundy wine) for 71F. The cooking is mostly macrobiotic style and 98% of ingredients are organic. Special diets, especially
vegan, can be catered for on request. No meat nor fish.
Also: take-away; health food shop; bookshop; cookery courses; dinner debates.

Thorenc

Plein Soleil

Guesthouse (board and lodging) Vegetarian
Plein Soleil
180 Chemin des quartre tours
06750 Thorenc.
Tel: 4 93 60 02 01
Approximately 50km north of Cagnes, by way of Vence and

Gréolières.
A haven for cures (slimming, health etc), training
courses (aromatherapy, kinesiology) or just for a relaxing stay,
Plein Soleil can also offer a meal for 80F. It is however
advisable to reserve the day before by telephone. Vegetarian
cuisine is served, in accordance with the dietary principles of
Dr Kousmine, with organic ingredients. Full board is around
360F single and 330F for a double, with a minimum stay of 3 days.

Tourettes-sur-Loup

La Nouvelle Aurore

Pension Vegetarian
La Nouvelle Aurore
306 Route des Virettes
06140 Tourettes-Sur-Loup.
Tel: 4 93 59 30 73 Fax: 04 93 59 25 56
North of Cagnes, via Vence. 1.5 km from Tourettes.
Peaceful, and with a view overlooking the sea, La Nouvelle
Aurore (The New Dawn) above all offers facilities for training
courses , but it is possible for individuals to stay too.
15 rooms are at your disposal. Single occupancy is 240 F full
board and 190 F half board. Of course the cooking is vegetarian, with
macribiotic food on request, made from 75% organic products,
notably the vegetables from the garden. The bread is home-made.

Ardèche 07

Devesset

Les Sapins

Guesthouse (board and lodging) Vegetarian
Les Sapins Devesset
07320 Saint-Agrève.
Tel/Fax: 04 75 30 06 05

Approximately 50km west of Valence, via Saint-Péray, Lamastre and
Saint-Agrève. Situated at an altitude of 1000m in the Ardèche mountains, the inn of Les Sapins offers a haven of relaxation and calm.
The house is surrounded by a park and equipped with a large wood-
en floored hall for training courses and conferences. Your stay can
be supplemented by yoga, local walks and relaxation, whether you
are here as an individual, part of a group or participating in a confer-
ence. The meals are served buffet-style and the cooking is vegetarian
and organic. Nancy and Stéphane Place recommend their vegetarian
speciality made from Auvergne cheese, fruit and vegetables as well
as international specialities. They promise to pay special attention to
new vegetarians who want to discover vegetarian cooking. Half
board costs 255-355F per person

Marcols-Les-Eaux

La Ferme Solaire

Guesthouse (board and lodging) Vegetarian
La Ferme Solaire Marcols-Les-Eaux
07190 Saint-Sauveur-de-Montagut.
Tel/Fax: 4 75 65 60 95
Approximately 20km north of Privas.
La Ferme Solaire (The Solar Farm) has 2 single and 4 double
rooms plus 2 cottages. It costs 270F a night for a double and
220F for a single. Breakfast 30F. 1850F for a week in one of
the cottages. All cooking is vegetarian. Lunch is 85F and
dinner is 98F. You need to make a reservation the day before.
It is possible to request meat, though why anyone except a tiger
would want to do anything so bizarre is beyond us.

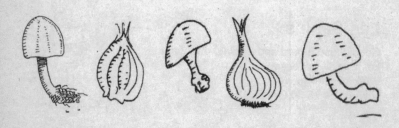

Aude 11

Rennes-le-Château

La Val Dieu

Guesthouse (board and lodging) Vegetarian
Pat Logan
La Val Dieu
11190 Rennes-leChâteau.
Tel: 4 68 74 23 21
25km south of Limoux. At Couiza, heading towards Quillan, take the D52 on the left to Rennes-le-Château. After 4 km turn left onto the road signposted La Val Dieu. La Val Dieu (The Valley of God) is a 50 hectare farm in the high Aude valley. Pat Logan offers full- and half-board accommodation supplemented by numerous activities such as rambling, yoga with the resident teacher, horse-riding and bird-watching. Reckon on paying 185F each per day half-board or 1165F for a week. All meals are vegetarian made with organic vegetables in season and dairy produce from the farm. Raw food diets and grape cures are also available. Also: camping (15F per person per night); yoga; horse-riding; bird-watching; rambling; farm work; visiting canyons; mountain biking.

Bouches-du-Rhône 13

Aix-en-Provence

Le Champignon

L'Arbre à Pain

Restaurant. Vegetarian friendly.
L'Arbre à Pain
12 rue Constantin
13100 Aix-en-Provence.
Tel: 4 42 96 99 95 Fax: 4 42 50 62 55
100m from the Law Courts.
Seats 34. Disabled access.

Open: 12.00-14.30 and 19.30-22.30 Tue-Sat. Closed for 2 weeks in August.
Credit cards accepted.
This vegetarian restaurant, situated in a lively little street in old Aix, offers two menus at lunchtime (75 and 110F) and one for dinner (110F) as well as à la carte (approximate cost 90F) in its large pastel-coloured dining hall. Annette Herna, the owner and cook, opened the restaurant 7 years ago and has created themed dishes, for example assiette méditerranéenne (mediterranean platter with hoummous, aubergine caviar and tapenade, which is olive paste), assiette gour-mande (gourmet platter with wheat escalopes and vegetables), assi-ette macrobiotique (macrobiotic platter), and assiette végétalienne (vegan platter). Children are not forgotten with ravioli and pizzeta (mini pizzas). On the tables are brown or wholemeal bread, gomasio, malted yeast, and tamari. All drinks (fruit juices, wine, cider, beer etc) as well as 95% of the produce, are organic. Also:take-away; book shop for cookery books; cookery courses.

Le Maharajah

Restaurant. Vegetarian-friendly.
Le Maharajah
16 rue des Tanneurs
13000 Aix-en-Provence.
Tel: 4 42 27 56 97
Open: every day except Monday lunchtime.
Top marks to this Indian restaurant which has a special vegetarian menu as well as a vegetarian platter for 145F per person.

Arles

Le Molière

Restaurant Vegetarian-friendly
Le Molière
H_tel de la Poste
2 rue Molière
13200 Arles

Cassoulet

Tel: 4 90 96 03 30 Fax: 04 90 49 80 28
This is the restaurant in the Hôtel de la Poste, near Van Gogh square.
Seats 40. Summer terrace. Parking.
Open: 12.00-14.30 and 19.00-22.30. Closed Monday. Closed 15
Nov- 15 Dec.
Credit cards: Visa, Amex
A traditional hotel-restaurant in an historic Napoleon III style
building, the interior hung with old local paintings. Over the
past 5 years, the manager, Élizabeth Clévenot, has developed an
original vegetarian menu which she still hopes to expand.
On the two fixed menus (72-98F) and the à la carte menu (approx
70F for a meal) vegetarians will find dishes such as La salade de
légumineuses aux algues (salad of pulses with seaweed), tarte aux
légumes (vegetable tart), tofu brouillé aux légumes (scrambled tofu
with vegetables), choucroute végétarien (vegetarian sauerkraut), tarte
aux noix (walnut tart). There is also semi-rye, walnut or cumin bread,
wine (organic or not), vegetable juices (10F) and tea (15F). About
50% of the produce is organic and the bread and tofu are home-
made. Vegans and those on macrobiotic diets can order specially
made dishes.
Also: hotel.

Vitamine

Restaurant. Vegetarian-friendly.
Vitamine
16 rue du Docteur Fanton
13200 Arles.
Tel: 4 90 93 77 36
Near to La Place du Forum.
Open: Mon-Sat lunchtime.
Vitamine has made salads their speciality. There are more than 50 on
the menu of which 5 or 6 are vegetarian (18-40F). There is also the
"Vitamine" platter for 65F made up of raw and cooked vegetables,
tofu and tamari. If you wish you can wash it all down with an organic
vegetable juice cocktail 20F.

La Baguette

Marseille

Auberge "In"

Restaurant. Vegetarian.
Auberge "In"
25 rue du Chevalier-Roze
13002 Marseilles.
Tel: 4 91 90 51 59
Near the Town Hall and Vieux-Port.
Open: 1200-1400 and 1900-2200 except Sunday and Bank Holidays.
Credit cards accepted.
Well situated in the heart of Marseilles,this strictly vegetarian restaurant offers a main course for 58F, a fixed menu for 75F (dish of the day plus fruit salad or chaocolate mousse and coffee) and an à la carte menu with dishes costing 50-70F. The bread, wine, vegetables and grains are all organic. Some macrobiotic dishes served. No meat nor fish.
Also: Take-away; health food shop.

Country Life

Restaurant. Vegan.
Country Life
14 rue Venture
13001 Marseilles
Tel: 4 91 54 16 44 Fax: 4 91 33 90 29
On the pedestrianized street between rue Paradis and rue Saint-Ferréol.
Métro: Estrangin.
Seats 70-100. Wheelchair access by lift. Non-smoking restaurant. Summer terrace.
Open: 1130-1430 Mon-Fri.
The restaurant only is closed for the first 3 weeks in August.
Credit cards accepted.
This large vegetarian restaurant is above the health food shop. The restaurant works as on a self-service basis where, for 58F, you select your own meal from a more than adequate choice of starters (more than 15 with 3 different sauces), and main

courses (couscous, lasagne, vol au vents, paella etc). If you
want you can finish off with a desert (15F) chosen from tartes
aux fruits (fruit tart), amandines (almond tart), fruits rouges
(red fruits) etc. Filtered water is served, as well as fruit juice (10F),
alcohol-free beer (12F), herbal teas or coffee substitute (5F). Make
the most of the different types of bread such as kamut bread, five
grain bread and rye bread. Children and students pay 35F.
Also: Take-away; health food shop; bookshop; cookery courses;
meetings on health with a nutritionist; stress management
courses.

La Manne

Restaurant Vegetarian-friendly
La Manne
18 boulevard de la Liberté
13001 Marseilles
Tel/Fax: 4 91 50 97 68
Near Saint-Charles station. Seats 106.
Open 1100-1600 Mon-Sat. Closed 1-15 August. Reservations
advisable.
Credit cards accepted.
In this large beamed room there is a choice of several main
courses at midday and in the evening, all at 50F. One selection is
specially for vegetarians: choice of starter, main course
gratin de boulghour (bulghur gratin), raviolis aux noix (walnut
ravioli). tomates farcies aux champignons (mushroom-stuffed
tomatoes) and cheese or dessert.
Also: Take-away; room for hire for functions.

Cantal 15

Le Falgoux

Le Tahoul

Guesthouse (board and lodging) Vegetarian
Le Tahoul
Michèle and Gilles Lanneau
15380 le Falgoux.
Tel/Fax: 4 71 69 51 67. Closed November or December.
From Aurillac (50km), Salers (15km) or Murat (30km), head
towards Puy Mary, le Falgoux. You will get to Le Falgoux through La
Chaze.
Chèques vacances (French luncheon vouchers) accepted.
In the heart of the Auvergne volcanic area, at an altitude of
1100m and in a conservation area, with incomparable views of the
high valley of the Mars an its circle of steep mountains. This is where
Michèle and Gilles Lanneau offer guest rooms and vegetarian food in
their large and pretty home built from
volcanic rock, which has been renovated with natural materials. 90%
of produce served is organic; salade exotique, seitan,
terrine de légumes (vegetable terrine), tofu croquettes,
spécialité auvergnate (speciality of the region made with
buckwheat flour, hot goat's cheese and walnuts), organic cheese,
mountain fruits etc. all accompanied by home-made organic bread,
moutain herbs (in the condiments or infusions), soya drinks and wine.
In fact, Michèle will cater for any request from her guests as long as it
is in accordance with vegetarian principles. For a stay of 3 days or
more you would pay 230F for full board or 175F for half-board for a 2
or 3 bedded room. If the dormitory is fine for you then take 20F off the
price.
Also: facilities for personal development courses and
conferences; rambling; cross-country skiing; winter walks on
snow-shoes.

olive

Thiézac

Le Clou

Guesthouse (board and lodging) Vegetarian-friendly
Le Clou
15800 Thiézac.
Tel: 4 71 47 01 45 Fax: 4 71 47 03 97
Thiézac is 26km north-west of Aurillac on the N122. Le Clou is
sign-posted from the cemetery in Thiézac.
Closed: 1st Nov-20th Dec.
Four Dutch people, Hennie, Franck and their two children, moved to
this natural volcanic park of the Auvergne in the heart of the Cantal
several years ago. The 19th century farm has been restored with
great taste. It is situated at an altitude of 1100m on the Elancèze
moutainside and offers rooms or a dormitory to stay in, vegetarian
and other food, and rambling or cross-country skiing. The atmosphere
is international. Expect to pay 1650F a week full-board and 1410F
half-board or slightly less for the dormitory. In the holiday cottage (4
bunk beds) expect to pay 81F per night bed and breakfast or 159F for
half-board. For vegetarian only food, advance notice is needed and a
small supplement is charged. You could be eating poires au bleu
d'Auvergne (pears with local blue cheese), quiche aux poireaux (leek
quiche), avocats au four (baked advocadoes), chou farci au tofu (tofu-
stuffed cabbage), lentil croquettes, semoule aux fruits de sureau
(semolina with elderberries), chocolate profiteroles, fresh fruit tart...
accompanied by rye bread, local spring water or wine (30F). Set
menu 80F.
Also: rambling; cross-country skiing; outings on snow-shoes.

Le vin

Drôme 26 4

Bellegarde-en-Diois

Le Gîte

Hotel-restaurant. Vegetarian.
Le Gîte Le Village
26470 Bellegarde-en-Diois.
Tel: 4 75 21 40 74 Fax: 4 75 21 40 56
Leave the A7 motorway at Bollène. Take the D94 to Nyons and
Rémuzat then north to Bellegarde-en-Diois on the D61. Seats 36.
Summer terrace. Parking.
Open: 1200-1400 and 1900-2100. From 5th January to 28th March
the restaurant is only open Friday lunchtime til Monday morning.
Reservations advisable on bank holidays and in the height of summer.
Situated between the rivers Diois and Drôme, at an altitude of 850m,
Le Gîte was established in 1977 and at the time advertised itself as
the premier strictly vegetarian hotel-restaurant in France. In
provençale surroundings there are three choices of meal for lunch
and dinner: a fixed menu at 85F; two dishes at 75F; and à la carte for
90-100F with for example salade de tomates à la tomme de chèvre
dite à la dioise (tomato salad with goats cheese Diois style for 20F),
seitan en brochettes garnie de légumes (seitan kebabs garnished with
vegetables for 50F), gâteau aux bananes (banana cake), or spiced
Linzer tart (15F). 70% of ingredients are organic particularly the
wholemeal bread and the drinks for example fruit juices and wine.
The Côtes-du-Rhône reserve from the Apollinaire vineyard costs 60F
and the Côtes-des-Baronnies from the Gautière vineyard is 61F.
Vegans and those on macrobiotic diets are well catered for. There is
a childrens menu for 40F, a large garden, table tennis, and a paddling
pool supplied by a pure spring. There is a great variety of mountain
landscapes and marked trails. Don't hesitate to ask for information
from the international staff. Also: hotel with 8 rooms and 4 appartments in the annexe; cookery courses; concerts and events.

Eygalayes

Ferme du Casage

Guesthouse. Vegetarian-friendly.
Ferme du Casage
26560 Eygalayes
Tel: 4 75 28 41 94 Fax: 4 75 28 42 73
About 30 km west of Sisteron. Head for Buis-les-Baronnies.
Isolated at a height of 850m in the grandiose landscapes of the
Haute-Provence, and turned towards the warm sun of Baronnies, this
ecological and alternative farm of 77 hectares was founded in 1983
according to bio-dynamic principles. Nature is respected and gives
the best of itself in return. Josette Fourmie runs with the restaurant
and serves you in a sunny dining room with a large veranda, with a
tiled floor and hemp on the walls and the ceiling. The food is simple,
country cooking, and the menu for the day lists crudités, vegetables
tarts, lasagnes ... with meals costing around 60F. Specify your prefer-
ences at the time of reservation.
It is also possible to stay for a longer time. There are 35 beds on
offer, divided over rooms, dormitories and two appartments.

Gard 30

Saint-Christol-lès-Alès

Association Santé et Vie

Boarding house vegetarian
Association Santé et Vie
Le Mas Perdu - Boujac
30380 Saint-Christol-lès-Alès.
Tel: 4 66 60 76 80
On the way out from Alès to Montpellier, Saint-Christol-lès-Alès
is only 5km away. To find Le Mas Perdu, take the old route from
Anduze till Boujac. Here you are welcomed on a farm, 100%
vegetarian and 100% organic. The bread is made on the spot, in a
wood oven. Vegans and those following a special diet will find appro-

priate dishes. Half board you pay 200F per person and per day
(370F for couples).
Other activities: cooking courses.

Hérault 34

Montpellier

Bio-Tea-Full

Restaurant. Vegetarian-friendly.
Bio-Tea-Full
3, rue Embouque d'or
34000 Montpellier.
Tel: 4 67 66 44 66
Between the Préfecture (regional government) and the place de la
Comédie. 10 minutes from the station.
32 seats.   Non-smoking.
Open fom 12 to 7pm - Closed on Sunday.
Credit cards accepted.
Bio-Tea-Full opened in January 1997. It is resolutely focused on products of organic agriculture. The meals are prepared with all the ingredients that are available from organic sources: grains, fruits, vegetables ... The cooking is not completely vegetarian but there are a lot of
veggie dishes. Every day there is a vegetarian dish, for example
lasagne with vegetables (50F) as well as a daily vegan delight, such
as broccoli tart with cereals (39F). Also every day a vegetable and
cereal based cake (un clafoutis). All dishes are served with crudités.
You will also find a choice of wines and fresh fruit or vegetable juices.
Other services: take away food - tea-room.

Le Coup de Pouce

Restaurant. Vegetarian.
Le Coup de Pouce
5, rue Lakanal
34090 Montpellier.
Tel: 4 67 72 63 41

Bus 5-6-2-11 ... (Louis Blanc station within walking distance)
Close to the Ursulines convent.
30 seats. Disabled access.
Open from 9am to 9pm. Tuesday to Saturday, and from 9am to 3pm
on Sunday.
Opened in 1996, this is the most recent vegetarian restaurant
in Montpellier. Le Coup de Pouce was founded on the initiative
of three members of the association "l'Attribut". The two cooks,
working in a kitchen which is visible from the dining room, prepare a
variety of organic family dishes which are strictly vegetarian. Every
day there is a tart, a salad (from 25F to 38F) and a hot dish (38F), for
example couscous with vegetables,curry with tofu, bulgur and
Chinese leaves. Also there is an à la carte menu and a choice of 6 or
7 salads, a red organic local wine at 20F for half a jug, fruit juices etc.
The restaurant, which is open throughout the day, has a tea-room in
the afternoon and breakfast from 9am; this can be simple (20F) or
complete (muesli, white cheese, honey) or can even include the
famous Budwig crème (32F).
Other service: take away food.

Tripti-Kulaï

Restaurant. Vegetarian.
Tripti-Kulaï
20, rue Jacques-Coeur
34000 Montpellier
Tel: 4 67 66 30 51 Fax: 4 67 40 47 06
Right next to the place de la Comédie.
44 seats. Non-smoking restaurant.
Open from 12 to 9pm, closed on Sundays - Closed during the last
three weeks of August. Credit cards accepted.
"Tripti-Kulaï" means nest of satisfaction in Bengali. The range
is quite impressive. In a stone-arched dining-hall, menus and cards
list vegetarian dishes from all over the world. You can have fritters
with feta cheese or guacamole vegetables; as a main, olive cake with
tomato sauce; end on a chocolat suprême or a cheesecake.
Everything accompanied by semi-wholemeal leavened bread with
leaven and other seasonings, tamari, yeast, gomasio. About 60% of
the ingredients are of organic origin. Vegans are also catered for on
request. Other activities: take away food, bookshop, cooking lessons.

Isère 38

Saint-Martin-de-Clelles

Ferme du Mont Inaccessible

Guesthouse. Vegetarian-friendly.
Ferme du Mont Inaccessible
Trézannes
38930 Saint-Martin-de-Clelles
Tel: 4 76 34 46 66. Fax: 4 76 34 48 52.
50km south of Grenoble, via the N75 towards Sisteron, near to Chichilianne.
Mr and Mrs Bichebois live on their farm, typical for the Trièves, in the middle of Vercors. They are happy to share their way of life and to explain their work as small organic farmers and breeders which they have been practising at this place for 20 years. In the vaulted eating-room (an old sheepfold) one or two menus from 75F to 120F are offered, consisting of green salad with warm goat's cheese, gratin of ravioli, blueberry tart, soft cheese with raspberry sauce. The products are, of course, from the farm. An organic wine is also on offer (from 25F to 75F). Obviously, non-vegetarians are also welcome. Allow 180F to 210F per person per night for half board. There is also the possibility of camping on the farm.
Other activities: take away food, bookshop.

Loire 42

Saint-Etienne

Les Oiseaux de Passage

Restaurant. Vegetarian-friendly.
Les Oiseaux de Passage
72, rue Antoine-Durafour

42100 Saint-Etienne
Tel: 4 77 37 54 44
Close to the Saint-Roch church. Bus 7-8.
40 seats. Non-smoking restaurant.
Open for lunch from Tuesday to Saturday. Also Friday and Saturday
evening. Tuesday, Wednesday and Thursday only open for groups if
booked. In an old chapel, with baroque decor, paintings and classical
music, this restaurant offers vegetable pâté, seitan etc, on a 73F set
menu including your choice of starter, main dish and a dessert.
Vegetables, grains and wine are 100% organic. Fish is also served.
Also take-away food.

Haute-Loire 43

Les Vastres

Le Lanteïrou

Guesthouse. Vegetarian-friendly.
Le Lanteïrou Champagne
43430 Les Vastres
Tel: 4 71 59 57 02
From Valence, head west towards Puy-en-Velay. Le Lanteïrou lies
between Saint-Agrève and Fay-sur-Lignon.
Closed during the November holiday of Toussaint. Near the Mont
Gerbier-de-Jonc is Jan Van Der Wijk's farm, built in basalt stone in
the sober and solid style of the plateau of Mézenc. This farm offers
accommodation in rural rooms and a vegetarian menu. 200F per night
for two persons, breakfast included and 70F per meal. Favourable
rates if you stay for more than three days half board (280F for two).
Le Lanteïrou has a large biological kitchen garden, and the vegetables from this garden are the basis of the fixed menu (70F, wine
included) on which you'll find crudités, potatoe pie, lasagne, fruit tarts,
crumbles, homemade icecream etc. A speciality is the cooking based
on wild plants. Cooking courses are organised if you wish to be
trained. 90% of the ingredients are biological. Bread, drinks and
liqueurs are homemade and the "tap" water comes from a mountain
spring. Vegans are catered for as far as possible. Sometimes meat

and fish are also served. Suitable dishes are available for children, who can also enjoy themselves around the farm.
Other activities: take away food (bio vegetables, jams, herbal teas), cooking courses (healthy cooking, bread making, cooking with wild plants).

Pyrénées (Orientales) 66

Serralongue

Douceur et Harmonie

Guesthouse. Vegan.
Douceur et harmonie
El-Faïtg
66230 Serralongue
Tel: 4 68 39 62 56
El-Faïtg (pronounced el Fatch) is an ancient stone farmhouse, with greenery on all sides, between the mountains, in 21hectares of grounds. The house has places for workshops in landscape architecture, as well as a contemplation space, and some simple rooms. The association was founded in 1964 with the aim of letting people know about veganism. It is also a "centre for the development of the gardenflowers of our souls, in order to prepare for a world of gentleness and harmony". Booking essential, charges are made according to financial means. The food is of course vegan and biological (garden crudités and basil sauce, buckwheat croquettes, mint tart, fruit jellies, raisin bread ...).
Other activities: Publication of the magazine Douceur et Harmonie, library, take-away food (homemade bread and garden vegetables).

Rhône 69

Lyon

Le Pâtisson

Restaurant. Vegetarian.
Le Pâtisson
17, rue Port-du-Temple
69002 Lyon
Tel: 4 72 41 81 71
Right in the centre, by the river near the Jacobins square.
Métro: Bellecour or Cordeliers. Bus 28, Jacobins station.
35 seats. Disabled access (except the toilets). Non-smoking restaurant.
Open from 11.30am to 2pm and from 7pm to 9.30pm. Closed Friday evening, Saturday noon and Sunday. Closed during the week of 15th August.
Booking always advised. Credit cards accepted.
During 15 years of classical cooking, Yves Perrin has been a finalist in numerous culinary competitions (Pierre Taittinger, Prosper Montagné and, for his 'nouvelle cuisine', Rebuchon).
Then he became vegetarian on principle and opened this restaurant in 1991. The building dates from the 15th century. At lunchtime he offers a daily special (50F), an à la carte menu (meals for around 80F) and 2 set menus (61F and 68F). In the evening there are two bigger menus for 85F and 100F, and an even

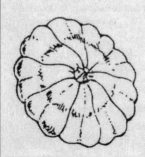

LE PATISSON

RESTAURANT VÉGÉTARIEN

17 RUE DU PORT DU TEMPLE
69002 LYON

04-72.41.81.71

more sophisticated à la carte menu.

The grilled specialities in the evening include tofu medallion "grand large" served with saffroned vegetable julienne (62F), "Potofu campagnard" (62F), "lugdunum" seitan escalope in beer with onions (62F). Also homemade cakes and pastries (18F), sorbets and ice-creams (20F), organic wines (18F for a glass), fruit or vegetable juices and cocktails (18F and 23F). 95% of the ingredients are of organic origin and the chef tries hard to to meet your dietary requirements: Kousmine, macrobiotic ... except meat and fish of course.

Other activities: take-away food

Savoie 73

Apremont

La Maison d'Apremont en Savoie

Guesthouse. Vegetarian-friendly.
La Maison d'Apremont en Savoie
Route du col du Granier
73190 Apremont.
Tel: 4 79 28 34 78 Fax: 4 79 28 25 43
About 10 km south from Chambéry, directly or via Challes-les-Eaux. Since 1988 Renée-Jeanne Dimier has been offering a vegetarian option including vegetable paté, soya steak or plum pudding. The meal will set you back 80F and a bottle of Apremont wine is 58F. For particular culinary needs please ask when booking. "Everything is possible" we have been told.

Also: take-away orders, bookstore, cuisine tuition,seminars, courses.

Chambéry 73

Aux Délices des Saison

Restaurant Vegetarian

Aux Délices des Saison
675 faubourg Montmélian
73000 Chambéry
Tel: 4 79 85 26 04
In the district Buisson-Rond near the swimming pool and the
Monge high-school.
24 seats, easy access for disabled people, non-smoking restaurant,
outdoor dining room in summer.
Open:11.30 to 3pm except Sunday, 7 to 9pm Monday and
Thursday. Closed from 15th to 30th of August. Booking advised.
Credit cards accepted.
Since November 1995 Chambéry has had its own vegetarian restaurant. Régine Hinniger has designed the decor: pale yellow fabric on
the walls, flowery tablecloths, green straw chairs, paintings and old
style plates. There are no menus, but a big card on which you will
find: hiziki 12F, pâté de soja accompagné de crudités (soya paté with
vegetables) 38F.... Dishes from 38 to 60F: vegetarian steaks, vegetable lasagne with green veg and mushrooms, sushi, mushroom
gougère, leek terrine. Of course, there is a choice of desserts, amandine aux poires (almond tart with pears) for 22F, tarte tatin for 18F.
All this is accompanied with wholemeal bread, gomasio, and a
good choice of organic drinks such as fruit juice (18F),
Beaujolais (58F), cider (48F). Almost all ingredients are organic, all
grains are whole grains and everything is home-made. Fish can also
be served.

Haute-Savoie 74

Ambilly

Le Temps de Vivre

Restaurant. Vegetarian-friendly.
Le Temps de Vivre
47 Chemin des Belosses
74100 Ambilly
Tel: 4 50 92 36 06
Near Annemasse.
Closed Sat lunchtime, Sun and Mon lunchtime.
A real vegetarian menu is on offer. For 150F you could start with vegetable carpaccio, soupe de courges à la farine grillée (squash soup
with toasted flour), risotto with boletus mushrooms, croustillant de
pommes de terre (shepherd's pie), quinoa, soja aux morilles (soya
with morel mushrooms), grilled tofu, followed by cheese and a dessert
of your choice.

Thonon-les-Bains

La Cassolette

Restaurant. Vegetarian-friendly.
La Cassolette
12 boulevard Georges-Andrier
74200 Thonon-les-Bains
Tel: 4 50 71 70 73. Next to the station towards Morzine-Avoriaz.
Seats 53. Summer terrace.
Open: 12.00-13.45 and 19.00-22.30. Closed on Monday.
Reservations advised at the end of the week.
Credit cards accepted (except American Express).
Not much in this region, so although La Cassolette gets a
mention because it uses organic products, it actually does not
offer a vegetarian menu but at least the vegetables will have
some taste. The owner is very helpful and will always find
something to cook from the organic shop next door.

Veyrier

L'Auberge de L'Eridan

Restaurant. Vegetarian-friendly.
L'Auberge de L'Eridan
13 Vieile Route des Pensières
74290 Veyrier
Tel: 4 50 60 24 00. Fax 4 50 60 23 63.
Near Annecy on the banks of the lake towards Thônes.
Wheelchair access. Parking.
Open: 12.00-14.00 and 19.30-21.30. Closed on Monday. Closed in
November and December.
In this three star Michelin, you can sample the cooking of Marc
Veyrat. There is no vegetarian menu as such but this great chef, well
known for his love of wild plants and flowers, offers several dishes
without meat and fish. For example? What would you say to soupe
de farine brûlée (soup with toasted flour), pimprenelle et truffes de
Savoie (burnet and truffle soup for 395F), or papillote de légumes
oubliés (forgotten vegetable parcels), sabayon liquide au goût de terre
(earthy sabayon 395F), or blanc manger d'ananas (pineapple blanc-
mange), accompanied by glace au romarin (rosemary ice-cream for
165F).

Var 83

Fréjus

L'Envol

Vegetarian fast food
L'Envol 408 rue Aubenas
83600 Fréjus
Tel 4-94 53 36 66 Fax 4-94 53 36 66
Opposite the Quadrillage stationery shop. L'Envol (the take-off)
is primarily a shop selling beautiful alternative items (crystals, hand-
woven garments, world music) which, since March 1997, also has
had a small snack bar and a 100% vegetarian take-away service.

Three or four tables are available for those wanting to eat a low-cost vegetarian meal on the spot. There are vegetable pasties (tartes aux légumes) are 12F, salads with sprouted seeds (salades à base de graines germées) about 12F a portion, tofu or seitan based dishes (plats à base de tofu, seitan), freshly pressed vegetable and fruit juices (jus de légumes et de fruits fraîchement préssés). By and large, everything is organic, but we couldn't find much for vegans in 1997. Also: a small shop selling natural produce.

Toulon

Le Maharajah

Restaurant. Vegetarian-friendly.
Le Maharajah
15 rue Emile-Gimelli
83000 Toulon
Tel 4-94 09 11 81
Closed Monday.
This Indian restaurant offers several dishes which are meat and fish-free, as well as a vegetarian platter or thali (plateau végétarien) at 145F.

Vaucluse 84

Avignon

Terre de Saveur

Restaurant. Vegetarian-friendly.
Terre de Saveur
1 rue Sain-Michel
84000 Avignon
Tel 4-90 86 68 72
Near the railway station, place des Corps-Saints
28 seats, disabled access, non smoking.
Open: 11.30-14.30 and from 15 June to 15 August also 19.00-21.30.

Closed Sunday and bank holidays. Annual closing mid February and mid August.

Reservations recommended. Credit card MC

This restaurant, opened in 1994, comprises two small rooms whose walls are used to hang the works of local artists. Élise Padilla, the chef, draws upon her 25 years experience of classical and vegetarian cooking to provide you with two set menus (68F and 78F) and an à la carte menu. Vegetarian specialities of the house include: aubergine with almond sauce (clafoutis d'aubergine à la crème d'amande) 45F, vegetable rosti with tahini sauce (rosti de légumes sauce tahin) 48F, chocolatine with candied ginger (chocolatine au gigembre confit) 28F. 90% of ingredients used are organic. Martine Pauron, the house manager, can also serve you with Lemaire bread (pain Lemaire), fresh vegetable and fruit juices (jus de légumes et de fruits frais), organic wine and beer (vins et bières bio), vegan dishes (plats végétaliens). Also: take-away.

L'Isle-sur-la-Sorgue

Le Basilic

Restaurant. Mainly vegetarian.
Le Basilic
9 quai Rouget-de-Lisle
84800 L'Isle-sur-la-Sorgue
Tel 4-90 38 39 84
10km north of Cavaillon or 22km east of Avignon. Near the Crédit Agricole bank.
35 seats in two rooms. Disabled access. Summer terrace. Parking.
Open 12.00-15.00 and in summer 19.00-23.00. Closed Thursday. Closed Dec-Jan. Reservations recommended in summer.

Marianne, who took over this restaurant in 1993, established a vegetarian regime also offering a single meat dish daily for non-vegetarians. In two bistro-style rooms, you can have the dish of the day for 49F or dine à la carte for about 150F, with numerous provençale specialities and Italian patés. You can choose from caponata 48F, salad with garlic and home-made olive paté (salad a l'ail et sa tapenade maison) 36F, courgette terrine in a fresh sauce (terrine de courgettes

et son coulis frais) 46F, Sicilian pesto (pesto à la sicilienne) 59F, farfale and devilled courgettes (farfale et courgettes à la diable) 65F,
tortellini in basil sauce (tortellini à la crème de basilic) 62F and a
choice of desserts for 28F such as pear clafoutis (clafoutis aux poires)
or crème caramel.

Sorgues

Pleine Nature

Restaurant. Vegetarian-friendly.
Pleine Nature
Centre commercial Avignon-nord
84700 Sorgues
Tel 4-90 32 65 333. Fax 4-90 32 82 6.1
Opposite the entrance to the Avignon-nord motorway, in the
Auchan-le-Pontet commercial centre, outside the covered market by
the cafe Le Grillon.
Pleine Nature is a mini-supermarket which includes a restaurant. The
food is organic and traditional. An entrée such as quinoa tabouleh
with basil (taboulé de quinoa au basilic), tarts, and cakes (gâteaux)
for 25F. Jean-Luc Sarritzu also offers a set vegetarian menu for 54F,
such as a platter with tempeh, small vegetables, crudités and quinoa.
Organic wine is 8F a glass, and a bottle of Côtes-du-Rhône costs
39F. Also: take-away, shop selling natural produce, a bookshop,
cookery courses and evening talks.

5. SOUTH WEST

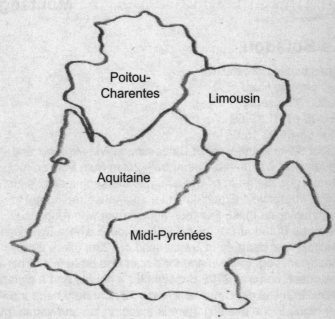

AQUITAINE
24 Dordogne, 33 Gironde, 40 Landes, 47 Lot et Garonne
64 Pyrénées-Atlantiques

LIMOUSIN: 19 Corrèze, 23 Creuse, 87 Haute-Vienne

MIDI-PYRÉNÉES
09 Ariège, 12 Aveyron, 31 Haute-Garonne, 32 Gers, 46 Lot
65 Hautes-Pyrénées, 81 Tarn, 82 Tarn et Garonne

POITOU-CHARENTES
16 Charente, 17 Charente-Maritime, 79 Deux-Sèvres
86 Vienne

Le Bufadou

Guesthouse. Vegetarian.
161 Grande Rue
09300 Montségur.
Tel: 05-61 01 19 59
Fax: 05-61 03 15 65
About 60km south-west of Carcassonne, via Mirepoix and
Lavelanet. It is on the Cathar trail, 20km from Foix on foot.
Montségur, the heart of Catharism in the Languedoc, is just the
place where we'd expect to find a vegetarian restaurant to
commemorate those fine men and women who renounced
meat. Le Bufadou is a typical village house where Raymond
Veullez, who came from Switzerland in 1990, offers a cos-
mopolitan, vegetarian menu for dinner and breakfast. There
are guest rooms at 210F per night for a double and a cottage
called L'Oustal del Caval which has 10 dormitory bed for 65F
per night. In the evening there is a vegetarian and vegan menu
for 80F which you should have booked when making your
reservation. Dishes include Salade Pic de la Mirandole followed by émincé de tofu à la hongroise (Hungarian minced
tofu), accompanied by quinoa and epeautre (another ancient
grain). For dessert there's homemade honey and pinenut par-
fait. For drinks choose from refreshing infusions (herb tea)
and fruit juices or you could have a bottle of wine (organic or
not) chosen by le patron (the owner) for 40F.
The ingredients, 60-80% organic, are local and some are actually picked on the property. Breakfast is 35F, with that French
health food speciality crème Budwig on request.
Also: reading room (some books for sale), concerts, meetings,
summer camp, exhibitions.

Aveyron 12

Ayssènes

Végétable d'Hôte

Guesthouse. Vegetarian.
Le Moulin
12430 Ayssènes.
Tel: 05-65 46 57 62
From Millau, follow the river Tarn west for about 40km, going
through Saint-Rome-de-Tarn and Pinet.
Ayssènes is a stone-built village of 35 inhabitants on a
promontary at the junction of two wild valleys. The mill is 200
metres below and as the access road is very narrow, it is best
to park your car in the village and help can be given with any
heavy luggage. The mill at Ayssènes is first and foremost a
vegetarian restaurant in an old stone house by the torrent, but
it is also a welcoming gîte offering full- and half-board accommodation. It costs 40F per night, 20F for breakfast, 140F half-
board.
Meals are cooked using vegetables grown in the terraced gar-
dens. 80% of the ingredients are organic. Maryvonne Jaffrelot
makes pâtés de soja (soya paté), beignets de légumes (vegetable fritters), la soupe de châtaignes (chestnut soup), seitan
sauté (sautéed seitan), bouquetières de légumes (vegetable
arrangement), savarins au thym (thyme savarin), daubes de
carrottes (carrot stew), topped off with homemade condiments.
The leavened bread is baked every week in their wood-burning
oven. There is also excellent spring water.
The set menu is 80F, drinks 15-50F. No meat, no fish, vegans
and health food freaks are well catered for as far as possible.
Also: rustic guest rooms with electricity provided by the
stream; cookery courses (two sessions a year); rambling; local
history.

Charente-Maritime 17

Aytré

La Source

Guesthouse. Mainly vegetarian.
Chez Anne et Charles Lucas
1 bis, boulevard Clemenceau
17440 Aytré
Tel: 05-46 44 57 86
Head towards Rochefort, after the Rochefort-Surgères roundabout turn right at the lights. Closed in July.
In rustic surroundings with a fireplace by the sea overlooking
an immense orchard, Anne Lucas offers a meal fo 50F at midday and in the evening. Specialities include crêpes aux
poireaux (leek crêpes), gâteau de fête aux lentilles et aux noix
(lentil and walnut celebration cake), pommes de terres aux
amandes (almond potatoes), soufflé au fromage (cheese soufflé), tarte aux pommes aux amandes et au miel (apple, almond
and honey tart), gâteau tiède aux épices douces (warm ginger-
bread), not to mention the macrobiotic specialities made from
tofu, tempeh, seitan and seaweed. Almost all ingredients are
organic. Fish and poultry are served on request. Also: cookery courses. Other events are planned for the future.

La Rochelle

Le Soleil Brille Pour Tout le Monde

Restaurant. Vegetarian-friendly.
Le soleil brille pour tout le monde
13 rue des Cloutiers
17000 La Rochelle
Tel: 05-46 41 11 42

In the centre of town, next to the market. Summer terrace.
Open: 12.00-14.00 and 19.30-22.00 Tue-Sat. Closes 22.30 in
summer and 23.00 on weekends.
Élisabeth Kamerbeck offers one or two specific dishes on her
menu from 39-60F. There is a vegetarian platter (mixed salad
with vegetable gratin and savoury pancakes) or savoury tart
served with green salad. You will also find semolina pancakes
and crêpes. Some ingredients are organic, notably the vegetables, flour and some oils. The wine comes direct from the pro-
ducers.

Corrèze 19

Estivaux

Les Rébières

Guesthouse. Vegetarian.
A.-M.Bugeat
19410 Estivaux
Tel: 05-55 73 77 55
On the Route Nationale 20 heading from Uzerche to Brive-la-
Gaillarde, turn right towards Perpezac-le-noir, then after the vil-
lage turn right again towards Estivaux. Opposite the stadium.
Situated in the middle of Corrèze, close to the canyons of
Vézère and Uzerche.
Madame Bugeat has owned this pleasant country house surrounded by an organic orchard for 24 years. She offers 4 guest
rooms in her house and two quaint gîtes, rated 3 stars by
Gîtes de France. Lunch (65 Francs), owing to the inspiration of
the cook, could be anything from a savoury fruitcake with
olives and pistachios (cake salé aux olives et aux pistaches),
cabbages stuffed with grain (chou farci aux céréales), gratins
or vegetable fritters (beignets de légumes), galettes served
with cep mushrooms, crêpes made of chestnut flour. Or if you

prefer to, choose the 35 Franc platter - ranging from a choice of crudités, cooked vegetables, cheeses and desserts.
Vegan and macrobiotic diets are not catered for here.
A single bedroom costs 200F per night, double 250F, triple 300F. Breakfast is especially filling and it is possible to order a Crème Budwig.

Sioniac

L'Espérance

Centre d'accueil (health farm). Vegetarian.
Barennal
19120 Sioniac
Tel/Fax: 05 55 91 08 54
L'Espérance (Hope) is a sanctuary for vegetarians situated near to Beaulieu-sur-Dordogne. Mr Deretz, who founded this place in 1974, derives great pleasure from providing information on the techniques and services offered: massage, balneotherapy, ozone therapy, fangotherapy (mud baths), iridology etc. The food is 95% organic and each meal is billed at 65 Francs. Vegans will find themselves particularly welcome.

Dordogne 24

Celles

Jane Edwards

Guesthouse. Vegetarian.
Pauliac
24600 Celles.
Tel: 05 53 91 97 45
Fax: 05 53 90 43 46
11 km north-east of Ribérac, in the Dordogne.

In this old farm nestled in the corner of a wooded valley, you can make the most of its tranquility, the small swimming pool and the vegetarian cooking. It costs 215F half-board and 255F full-board. Garden vegetables in season. Jane can also cater for non vegetarians by prior arrangement.

Champagnac-de-Belair

La Roche

Guesthouse. Vegetarian.
24530 Champagnac-de-Belair.
Tel: 05-53 54 22 91
35 km north of Périgueux, via Brantôme. The house and guest rooms are in an old barn, the gîte (for 8 people) is in an old farm. La Roche offers the charm of English hospitality with a swimming pool in summer. The meals are vegetarian and cost, including wine, 80F. Breakfast is 25F. Vegans meals are possible on request. The lady of the house uses mostly garden vegetables. There are two double rooms for 140-185F per night. Deduct 10% for winter periods or stays of more than 6 nights.

Château-l'Évêque

La Chabrerie

Maison de repos (rest house). Vegetarian.
Château-l'Évêque
24460 Agonac
Tel/Fax: 05 53 46 34 91
About 10km north of Périgueux.
This vegetarian retreat is in a château right in the middle of a park. It has been registered by the French Social Security and offers healthy eating stays, relaxation courses and vegetarian cookery courses. The rest home has 19 beds and an overnight stay including full board and events costs 290F for a single

and 200F for a double. Guests on average stay 3 weeks but you can also come and have a vegetarian meal for 55F at lunchtime and 45F for evenings.

Plazac

Le Moulin de Mayence

Restaurant. Vegetarian-friendly.
24580 Plazac
Tel: 05-53 50 55 52
From the N89, between Brive-la-Gaillarde and Périgueux, head south for 15km in the valley of the Vézère towards Montignac. At Thonac turn right towards Plazac.
4 small rooms.Summer terrace.
Open from Easter to November. Closed Monday, Tuesday and Wednesday evenings. Credit cards accepted.
As the name suggests, this is an old mill. The lock is closed but the spring water crosses the four small rooms of the restaurant and you can see fish swimming in it. Outside there are games for children and a lovely terrace shaded by weeping willows. Further away there is the valley of Vézère with its famous prehistoric sites.
Although this is a traditional restaurant there are many vegetarian clients which is perhaps partly explained by the nearby active Tibetan centre. There is a choice between a menu at 80F (soup, entrée, main dish,cheese and dessert), a range of pizzas from 38-45F or dishes chosen from the menu such as hot goat's cheese salad, feuilleté au crottin de chavignole (chavignole cheese parcels), truffle omelette, tofu burgers.

Saint-Vincent-Jalmoutiers

Le Vieux Four (The Old Oven)

Guesthouse. Vegetarian.
Saint-Vincent-Jalmoutiers
24410 Saint-Aulaye
Tel: 05-53 90 44 82
60 km west of Périgueux, by Ribérac.
An Englishwoman, Jane Moffatt, offers three guest rooms for
200F a night with breakfast, in her lovely old Périgord house
with wooden beams and stone walls, huge fireplace and traditional bread oven.
Half board includes the evening meal and if you want vegetarian meals you should mention that at the time of reservation. A
meal costs 95F.

Haute-Garonne 31

Saint-Gaudens

Cuisine et Santé

Guesthouse. Vegetarian.
Pont de Valentine
31800 Saint-Gaudens
Tel: 05-61 89 75 14. Fax: 05 61 89 36 07.
From Saint-Gaudens head for Luchon.
Open throughout year. Meals from 7 to 9am, 12.45 to 1.30pm
and 7.45 to 8.30pm. Advance booking advised for groups.
Cuisine et Santé is the most important macrobiotic centre in
France. Each meal is preceded by cooking lessons, accompa-
nied by explanations given by René Lévy - founder of the firm -
who has 10 years experience at the side of macrobiotic guru
George Ohsawa and his wife Lima.

The price of a stay, which includes the practice of macrobiotic cooking, accommodation, food and the classes is 200F per day with single room, 170F double and 140F in the dormitory. You can also come to discover the basics of Yin and Yang over a meal for 30F.

Fish is served on Fridays. Ingredients are of organic origin and the cooking is done in accordance with macrobiotic rules (cutting of vegetables, roasting of food, balance of acids and bases). The cooks use the complete range of macrobiotic foods: seaweed, whole grains, seitan, uméboshi....

Sauveterre-de-Comminges

Le Clos Saint-Michel

Boarding house. Vegetarian.
Bruncan
31510 Sauveterre-de-Comminges
Tel: 05-61 88 32 28
At 10km south of Saint-Gaudens, via Valentine.
Open from 1st April to 30th September. Booking essential.
This boarding house occupies a restored bourgeois house, south facing on 2 hectares of land and woods. 9 rooms are at your disposal. 240F for full board for a single person or 420F for couples. For half board you will pay 200F for a single and 330F for a double room. Meals are vegetarian and are prepared with 50% of the ingredients organic.

Toulouse

Bioasis

Restaurant. Vegetarian.
21, rue des Amidonniers
31000 Toulouse
Tel: 05-61 13 99 67
Fax: 05-62 27 00 12
Close to the Pont des Catalans
Métro place de la République (Saint-Cyprien).
Bus no. 1.
100 seats. Non-smoking restaurant. Parking for 5 cars.
Open from 12 to 2 or 3pm, Tuesday to Saturday.
Closed from 1st to 15th August. Credit cards accepted.
This restaurant, which opens at noon, is run by a cooperative
that grew out of an association of consumers of organic products, and which is very active in the field of ecology.
Meals cost between 55 and 65F, but you may also have a dish
of the day a là carte (45F) or a complete meal for about 100F.
99% of the ingredients used are of organic origin. The water is
purified by osmosis. Vegans will easily find a suitable meal.
Other activities: take-away food, health food shop, bookshop,
cooking courses, talks on organic agriculture and ecological
living.

Le vin

Grandeur Nature

Restaurant. Vegetarian.
21, avenue des écoles Jules-Julien
31400 Toulouse
Tel: 05-61 53 95 63. Fax: 05-61 32 89 44.
In the Rangueil quartier, opposite the theatre Jules-Julien.
Entrance via the west circular road (rocade), taking the Busca
exit. 80 seats. Parking.
Open only for lunch 12 to 2.30pm, Mondays to Fridays.

Credit cards accepted (CB, V).
This restaurant, opened in 1991, is run as a co-operative.
It is situated in the basement of a health food shop, but the
opening on a garden permits a clear view. You eat in a pan-
elled setting, surrounded by the green of the plants, at a table
cut out of a large tree trunk. The formula is original, very free
and flexible: self service by weight. You create your own
menu, choosing from two tables, one hot (cooked tofu,
steamed vegetables, pulses, grains, cereal burgers etc), the
other cold (salads, eggs, sprouted grains, vegetable paté etc).
You then have it all weighed (120F per kilo). The total will
come to about 50 to 60F per meal.
Don't forget the fruit purée, flan, yoghurt, cheese, or home-
made pastries which will be billed by the item, like the drinks. It
seems that it is possible to obtain fish or meat accompanied by
vegetables on request.
Other activities: take away food, health food shop, bookshop,
cooking courses. The association arranges entertainment
throughout the year.

Gironde 33

Bordeaux

Malabàr

Restaurant. Vegetarian-friendly.
7, rue des Ayres
33000 Bordeaux
Tel: 05-56 52 18 19
Between the town hall and quays (close to parking Victor-
Hugo). Three rooms, one of which is reserved for non-smok-
ers. 48 seats. Disabled access.
Open from 12 to 2pm and from 7.30 to 10.30pm, Tuesday to
Saturday. Closed in August. Booking recommended for end

of the week.
Credit cards accepted (CB, V, AE).
Nicole Taillade, cook and owner, got turned onto vegetarian
and Indian cooking 14 years ago by Guy Waelter, of the Manali
restaurant, who used to be a veritable oracle on the matter.
The only thing she needed to do was to start on her own,
which she did in 1985 when the Malabàr was born .
There are vegetarian menus (45F and 65F at noon, wine or
coffee included; 72F in the evening), or eat à la carte (meals
from 80F to 100F) and choose, for example, samosa with vegetables (30F), vegetable curry with whole grains and saffron
(34F), carrot and pistachio halva (18F), rice cream with rose-
water (16F). In the evening, the Indian bread (chapati) is
homemade. The wholegrain is organic. Water of course (filtered with Filopur) a wine list, bio or not (from 50F to 70F),
lassi (16F and 17F), fruit kéfir (15F), tea.
Other activities: take away food, groceries (saffron from
Aquitaine, kéfir), shop (fabric from Pondichery and Indian craft-
work), Indian cultural association (tickets on sale at the time of
the festivities).

Landes 40

Mont-de-Marsan

Gandhi

Restaurant. Vegetarian-friendly.
Gandhi
28bis, place Joseph-Pancaut
40000 Mont-de-Marsan
Tel: 05-58 85 97 97
Open 7 days a week. There is a menu for 87F, which lists
(among others) vegetarian starters and mains. Note that à la
carte you can eat vegetarian for less than that.

Lot 46

Cahors

Marie Colline

Restaurant. Vegetarian.
173, rue Clemenceau
46000 Cahors.
Tel: 05 65 35 59 96
In the town centre, close to the covered market.
50 seats. Non-smoking restaurant. Summer terrace.
Open from 12 to 2pm Tuesday to Saturday.
Closed in August. Booking advised.
This restaurant was founded 15 years ago and the present
owner offers you 2 menus at 38F (one dish) and 80F to show
you family vegetarian cooking. The desserts are home-made,
wine is served (14F for half a litre), as well as fruit juices (7F),
cider and beer. Neither meat nor fish.
Other service: take-away food.

L'Orangerie

Restaurant. Vegetarian.
41, rue Saint-James
46000 Cahors
Tel: 05-65 22 59 06
In the town centre, close to the cathedral.
45 seats inside, 30 terrace seats.
Open at noon and in the evening, from Tuesday to Saturday.
Closed during the Christmas holidays.
In the Orangerie you can eat vegetarian in a very light dining
room, well illuminated by a picture window, or even better, during the summer, on a terrace with wisteria in a very peaceful
courtyard. You will be offered pancakes, bricks, vegetable
curry served with bread and wine of organic origin, just like

the majority of the ingredients.
Everything is offered in the form of two menus for 68F and
98F. The plat du jour costs 42F.
Other activities: take away food.

Lot-et-Garonne 47

Bazens

Le Marchon

Guesthouse. Vegetarian.
Le Marchon
Bazens
47130 Port-Sainte-Marie.
Tel: 05-53 87 22 26 Fax: 05 53 87 22 26
email: 101530.1437@compuserve.com
About 20km west of Agen, on the N113, towards Bordeaux.
Le Marchon is a large country house, surrounded by cedars,
lime trees and hundred-year-old oaks, with a view of the vineyards and the Garonne valley.
Luc Smets offers you a half-board stay for 175F per person in
one of his 5 guest rooms. He puts at your disposal a large living room with fireplace, a swimming-pool, a piano, a sculpture
workshop and even the advice of a sculptor.
The meals are vegetarian and as far as possible with produce
from the region. The organic wholemeal bread with leaven is
homemade, as are the jams. The vineyard provides grapes for
the table and grapejuice.
Special diets are catered for. Once or twice a week fish is also
served.

Bouglon

Domaine de Montfleuri

Guesthouse. Vegetarian.
Doma Dominique Baron
Domaine de Montfleuri
47250 Bouglon
Tel: 05-53 20 61 30
15km south of Marmande. Take the D933 between
Casteljaloux and Marmande. Turn off towards Bouglon. The
Domaine de Montfleuri is 1.5 km from Bouglon, towards
Guérin.
At the boundaries of Périgord, Bordelais, Gironde and the forest of Landes, the Domaine de Montfleuri accommodates you
in guest rooms: 450F per person for a weekend (2 nights) in a
room for 3 to 4; 1600F for a week (7 nights). The vegetarian
meals are mostly prepared with vegetables from the garden.
During your stay you can enjoy the landscaped park, the swimming pool, as well as numerous activities such as rambling,
painting and table tennis.
You can have your meals inside the 13th century building or on
the flower terrace. For 100F, wine included, you can eat such
things as asparagus casserole , prune and bean stew, gratins,
vegetable lasagne, fruit granités (ice cream) or other home-
made pastries.
If you are interested in organic gardening and vegetarian cooking, Dominique Baron will even invite you to participate in the
garden or kitchen work.
Other activities: cooking courses are possible.

La Baguette

Cassoulet

Pyrénées Atlantiques 64

Oloron-Sainte-Marie

La Bio Assiette

Restaurant. Vegetarian.
4, avenue Charles-Moureu
64400 Oloron-Sainte-Marie
Tel: 05-59 39 65 23
Fax: 05-59 39 67 93
At the end of the Aspe valley and of Somport, 30 minutes
south of Pau, head for Saragosse; the restaurant is in the
square of Oloron park. 20 seats. Disabled access. Non-
smoking restaurant. Summer terrace. Open from 12 to 3pm,
Tuesday to Saturday. Booking advised.
This 100% vegetarian restaurant is an integral part of the small
organic supermarket, l'Epicerie verte. Manager Yann Charon
tries hard to let his clients discover a variety of vegetarian
foods by preparing forgotten vegetables, and unknown or exotic ingredients. The products are of course of organic origin,
and the cooking is inspired by macrobiotics. Practically all
dishes are suitable for vegans.
The prices are low, the plat du jour changes every day, there is
a fixed price menu at 60F and an à la carte menu for about
80F, varying according to the day and the season. Some specialities: vitamin salad, soft pumpkin with azukis and quinoa,
rice burgers with pear compote ... everything accompanied by
sesame bread, water from the Mont-Roucous, gomasio,
tamari, yeast flakes. Drinks available: fruit juice, grain coffee,
beers and organic wine by the jug (16F) or the bottle (from
45F).
Other activities: health food sho, bookshop, cooking courses
and entertainment in various forms, organised by Potimarron
alternative association.

Deux-Sèvres 79

Coulonges-sur-l'Autize

Marie Reisler

Guesthouse. Vegetarian.
27 rue du Commerce
79160 Coulonges-sur-l'Autize
Tel: 05-49 06 03 87
22km north of Niort on the D744. In the centre of town near
the market place.

Marie Reisler is the co-founder of the "Alliance Végétarienne"
and invites you to share her idea of varied and tasty cruelty-
free cooking. Take advantage of your visit to also browse in
her library which is well stocked with books on the subject.

The house is 15km from the Poitiers marshes, in the middle of
the village. For half board, allow 135F per person per day.
Room only 70F for one person, 120F for a couple and 160F for
three persons. Add 15F for breakfast.

Food is exclusively vegetarian and in summer is served on the
terrace: cereal burgers (galettes de céréales), vegetable pies
(tartes aux légumes), and vegetables au gratin (gratins aux
légumes), prepared with organic ingredients and accompanied
by wholemeal bread. The meal costs 70F and includes organic wine. The meal can be altered to suit your requirements
and can be vegan.

Also: shop selling natural produce and a bookshop.

La Bière

Le vin

Tarn 81

Albi

Le Tournesol

Restaurant. Vegetarian.
11 rue de l'Ort-en-Salvy
81000 Albi
Tel: 05-63 38 38 14
In the centre of town, near the place du Vigan.
1 smoking room, 1 non-smoking room. Seats 50. Wheelchair access. Summer terrace.
Open: 12.00-14.00 Tuesday-Saturday and 19.00-21.30 Friday and Saturday. Credit cards: V, AE
Sally Pignet chose a modern and bright environment in which to open her restaurant over ten years ago. She offers strictly vegetarian dishes which, Sally says, should appeal to everyone - not merely to the initiated. No set menus but four original, wholesome dishes 46F: l'assiette Tournesol (vegetable pâté, two hot corn burgers, crudités and green salad), assiette du jour (pumpkin flan, quinoa with grilled almonds, crudités and green salad), l'assiette fermière (farmhouse platter) ....
There are also à la carte hot dishes which change every day and vary according to the season: vegetables au gratin (gratins de légumes), cereal fritters (croquettes de céréales), savoury pasties (tartes salées), and a choice of desserts at 25F, such as hazelnut galettes with pear custard (galette de noisettes avec crème anglaise aux poires) or apple, banana and cherry tart (tourte pomme-banane-cassis). Wholemeal bread, malted yeast and gomasio are on the tables.
Beverages include organic wine (vin bio) at 40F a bottle, 10F a quarter litre, fruit juice (jus de fruits) at 12F, beers and herb teas (infusions). About 25% of ingredients are organic. Some dishes are vegan.

Lugan

La Source

Guesthouse. Vegetarian.
Les Cleris
81500 Lugan
Tel 05-63 41 88 51
Fax 05-63 40 07 65
Leave Toulouse on the N88 towards d'Albi. After about 30km
trun towards Lavaur. Lugan is on your right, 5km after Saint-
Suplice-sur-Tarn.
Here is a society with a humanitarian goal (action in Africa),
which offers food and lodging in a large country house beside
an orchard. There are five bedrooms, with a library on the
same floor which is open to guests, and a meditation room
which you may also use.
Half board is 200F per person, or 150F in a double room.
Meals cost between 45F and 80F and are always meat and
fish-free made with organic ingredients. For example spiced
raw vegetables (crudités aux épices), polenta or couscous with
vegetables (couscous aux légumes).
There are also a bookshop, library, cookery courses, workshops, exhibitions.

Tarn-et-Garonne 82

Montauban

La Clef des Champs

Restaurant. Vegetarian.
3 rue Armand-Cambon
82000 Montauban
Tel 05-63 66 33 34

Near the church of Saint-Jacques.
42 seats, no smoking.
Open from 11.45, closed Sunday. Closed August.
Reservations recommended.
The chef Anne-Marie Levau, who opened this restaurant in
1984, offers her mainly female customers a strictly vegetarian
family cuisine. Anne-Marie uses at least 70% organic produce
and a wide variety of spices. She offers goat's cheese salad
(salade au fromage de chèvre), the house speciality,
Vietnamese pancakes - banh xao to purists (crêpe vietnami-
enne) and a choice of 5 or 6 homemade pastries (pâtisseries
maisons). Allow 77F for a meal.
Beverages include fruit juice (jus de fruits) 13F, organic wine
(vin bio) 13F a quarter litre, cider, mineral waters.
Also: take-away.

Haute Vienne 87

Limoges

La Parenthèse

Restaurant. Vegetarian-friendly.
Cour du Temple
22 rue du Consulat
87000 Limoges
Tel 05-55 33 18 25
Near the parking by the covered market.
40 seats with a smoking and a no-smoking room.
Open: Tue-Sat 12.00-19.00
This traditional restaurant places great emphasis on vegetables. Vegetarians will have no difficulty in finding something to
eat, for example pies 38F, vegetable terrines plus salad (terrines de légumes servies avec une salade) 40F, mixed salad
(salades composées)45F.

Also: take-away to order.

Nouic

La Guyonnerie

Guesthouse. Vegetarian.
Vivien Hale
La Guyonnerie
Nouic
87330 Mezieres-sur-Issoire
Tel 05-55 60 23 75
About 40km north of Limoges, either via Bellac (N147) or via
the historic villages of Oradour-sur-Glane and Mortemart
(N141). La Guyonnerie is an old farm set in a small hamlet of
just ten families. There is a pond, lots of space, calm and an
English welcome on offer. Vivien Hale has four guest rooms
and serves meals which never contain meat or fish. A family
room (for a couple, a child and a baby) costs 195F a night.
If you require vegan or macrobiotic food you have only to ask.
Meals cost just 40F, and 20F for children.

Saint-Pardoux

Château de Vauguenige

Restaurant. Vegetarian-friendly.
87250 Saint-Pardoux
Tel 05-55 76 58 55
Leave the N20 at Razes, 25km from Limoges, and head for
Saint-Pardoux. Follow the directions for Bessives, then
Rancon and Saint-Symphorien., Vauguenige will be on the
right. 25 seats, summer terrace.
Open 12.30-14.00. Open every day during school holidays,
but only Fri evening to Sunday outside the holidays. Closed
Nov-April. Reservations required.
Marick and Alain Claude offer you a luxururious nineteenth

century castle residence set in an estate of 9 hectares, complete with covered swimming pool. The guest rooms were opened in 1988. The food was originally macrobiotic but the choice has since been widened and Marick Claude now offers vegan and vegetarian meals as well as meat and fish dishes. The restaurant is open to non-residents. Brunch is available Sunday mornings from 10.30 to 12.30. The two set menus for 96F and 132F include wood-smoked tofu terrine (terrine de tofu fumé forestière), Thai tempeh (tempeh à la thaïlandaise), nut fritters (des croquettes aux noix), chocolate cake with vanilla sauce (du gateau au chocolat et sa sauce vanille). 25 to 30% of ingredients are organic. There is a wine list and a choice of fruit juices.

Also: take-away on request.

CONTACT FELLOW VEGGIES IN FRANCE

If you're in France for a long time, here are some French organisations to join and make new friends, or get active in. Send a stamp or international reply coupon for details in French. *Please remember these are hard-pressed charities campaigning to make France safe for animals and they cannot answer letters in English and certainly don't provide school project or tourist info.* But they welcome your leftover French money!

Action Information pour les Droits des Animaux (AIDA), c/o MBE no 200, 117 bd Voltaire, Paris 75011. Inspired by the UK Vegetarian Society and Animal Aid, promoting vegetarianism especially to the young.

Aequalis Animal, 12 rue du Fief, 92100 Boulogne-Billancourt. Tel 01 46 21 08 03, Fax 01 46 21 44 98. CCP 40 467 48 E - La Source. Inspired by PETA with a high media profile, campaigning for vegetarianism and animal welfare. No group has had a bigger impact, with spectacular TV successes exposing, for example, BSE and making vegetarianism cool for the first time in France. 100F annual subscription, plus 60F to receive their quarterly magazine.

Alliance Végétarienne, Beauregard, 85240 Saint-Hilaire-des-Loges. Tel 05 49 06 03 87. Magazine, books, recipes, meetings. 120F subscription.

Les Amis de la Terre, 53 rue Ramus, 75020 Paris. Tel 01 43 49 11 00.

LAFDAM (Ligue Antivivisectioniste de France, Défense des Animaux Martyrs), 39 rue Caulaincourt, 75018 Paris. Tel 01 42 64 46 54.

SUNFLOWER WORLD WIDE VEGETARIAN RESTAURANT GUIDE

VEGETARIAN FRANCE
READER RESPONSE FORM

We are relying on **YOU** to help make the next edition of *Vegetarian France* even better. The best letters will receive a free copy of your choice of one of our guides. Please feel free to continue on as many sheets as you wish. Merci beaucoup.

Are there any improvements you'd like to see in the guide?

Any places you would like to see featured in the next edition?

Any places you would like to see chopped out of the next edition, and why?

Any descriptions you would like to see changed?

Where did you buy your guide? _____

Are you: veggie __ vegan __ other _____

Your name: . . . .

Address: . . . .

. . . .

. . . . Postcode . . . .

Please return to: Vegetarian Guides Ltd, 32 Brading Rd, London SW2 2AW.

VEGETARIAN
BRITAIN

By Alex Bourke and Alan Todd
Foreword by Paul and Linda McCartney

Hankering for a day trip or weekend away and wondering if you should pack a hamper first? Now you can dump the veggie emergency kit, safe in the knowledge that wherever you go, you'll be able to refuel at totally vegetarian and vegan eateries and sleeperies.

This brand new guide features **hundreds of vegetarian restaurants, cafés, hotels and guest houses all over Britain with opening times, prices and full descriptions including what's on the menu for vegans. The most up-to-date, comprehensive and detailed veggie guide ever.**

Available from bookshops, price £7.99.
Or order direct from Vegetarian Guides Ltd, 32 Brading Rd, London SW2 2AW.

Credit card orders telephone the Vegetarian Society on 0161-928 0793.

- -

Name: . . . .

Address: . . . .

. . . .

Postcode . . . . Telephone: . . . .

Please send me ...... copies of *Vegetarian Britain* @£7.99, ... copies of *Vegetarian France* @£6.99, ... copies of *Vegetarian Oz/NZ* @£4.99, ... copies of *Worldwide Vegetarian Guide* @£9.99. Postage and packing: one book add £1.50, then £1 per book. For postage to EC: add 50% of total book order. Other countries add 100% of total book order.
Total for items listed above £ ...... Postage £ ...... TOTAL £ ....
Make cheques/PO payable to Vegetarian Guides Ltd. Sterling payment only.